Desserts
on the Mediterranean

Desserts
on the Mediterranean

Sweets and Treats Inspired by
the Mediterranean Diet

VERONICA MILES

peapil

PEAPIL PUBLISHING
PO Box 65460
Salt Lake City, Utah 84165
www.peapil.com

Copyright © 2022 by Peapil Publishing

All rights reserved. Except as permitted under the U.S. Copyright Act of 1976, no part of this publication may be reproduced, distributed, or transmitted in any form or by any means, or stored in a database or retrieval system, electronically or otherwise, or by use of a technology or retrieval system now known or to be invented, without the prior written permission of the author and publisher.

Interior by Ashley Tucker
Cover Design by Ashley Tucker
Contributions by Kirsten Armstrong
Culinary Photography by David E. Carranza Calvillo
Food Styling by Itze McConnehey

First Edition

Contact the author at support@peapil.com

Paperback ISBN: 979-8375814-14-8
eBook ISBN: 978-1-990281-55-6
Audiobook ISBN: 978-1-990281-56-3

Disclaimer
All material on Peapil.com and in this book is provided for your information only and may not be construed as medical advice or instruction. No action or inaction should be taken based solely on the contents of this information; instead, readers should consult appropriate health professionals on any matter relating to their health and well-being. If you think you may have a medical emergency, call your doctor or 911 immediately.

The content of this book (text, graphics, and images) is not intended to be a substitute for professional medical advice, diagnosis, or treatment. Always seek the advice of your physician or other qualified health provider with any questions you may have regarding a medical condition.

Never disregard professional medical advice or delay in seeking it because of something you have read in this book. The information and opinions expressed here are believed to be accurate, based on the best judgment available to the authors. Readers who fail to consult with appropriate health authorities assume the risk of any injuries. Reliance on any information and content provided by Peapil Publishing and this book is solely at your own risk.

The publisher is not responsible for errors or omissions.

Contents

Introduction ——————————————————————————— 9

The Mediterranean Approach ————————————————— 11

Desserts the Mediterranean Way ———————————————— 14

Ingredients and Substitutions ————————————————— 15

   Chocolate   Butter

   Substitutions   Eggs

   Fruit   Dairy

   Nuts and Seeds   Lactose Intolerant/Vegan Alternatives

   Olive Oil   Sweeteners

Why Do We Get Cravings? ——————————————————— 20

   Cravings versus Hunger   Psychological Causes

   Physical Causes

Gaining Control ——————————————————————— 24

Do Desserts Have Health Benefits? ——————————————— 26

Mediterranean Desserts ———————————————————— 29

Main Desserts

- Honey Pecan Mascarpone Cups
- Banana Pistachio Oatmeal Cookies
- Chocolate Apricot Pudding
- Four Ingredient Tahini Nut Fudge
- Chocolate Apricot Truffles
- Roasted Apricots
- Chocolate Hummus
- Pistachio Ice Cream
- Lemon Thyme Coconut Ice Cream
- Roasted Fruit Medley
- Greek Almond Cookies (Amygdalota)
- Mandarin Orange Galette
- Fig Walnut Bundt Cake
- Cranberry Mandarin Orange Bread
- Maple Fig Shortbread Tart
- Pistachio Pomegranate Loaf
- Chocolate Avocado Mousse
- Mango Mousse
- Clementine Coconut Panna Cotta
- Clementine Peach Crumble
- Peach Apricot Sherbet
- No-Bake Mediterranean Lemon Pie
- Apricot Macaroons
- Mediterranean Crêpes
- Spiced Orange Ricotta Cake
- Brûléed Berry Mascarpone
- Baked Plums with Pecans & Maple Syrup
- Olive Oil Pecan Banana Bread
- Greek Milk Pie (Galatopita)
- Carrot Cake
- Grapefruit Lavender Olive Oil Cake
- Almond Olive Oil Shortbread Crackers
- Cranberry Almond Biscotti
- Moustokouloura Cookies
- Maple Date Cake
- Baked-Apple Baklava
- Sardinian Almond Cake
- Lemon Olive Oil Pound Cake
- Revani Cake (Basbousa)
- Spanish Almond Cookies (Almendrados)
- Peach Crumb Tart
- Loukoumades (Greek Honey Balls)
- Mediterranean Rice Pudding
- Olive Oil Cornmeal Cookies
- Maple Orange Phyllo with Spiced Fruit
- Crème Brûlée
- Toasted Coconut Cornmeal Cake
- Spiced Red Wine Cookies
- Tahini Brownies
- Greek Bougatsa with Honey & Pistachios
- Pistachio Pudding
- Fig Walnut Cookies
- Apricot Clafoutis
- Spiced Walnut Fruitcake
- Italian Lemon Ricotta Cookies
- Middle Eastern Halva Shortbread
- Date Almond Brownies
- Lebanese Semolina Pudding
- Olive Oil Chocolate Chip Cookies
- Pear Frangipane Tart
- Roasted Fig & Apricot Gelato
- Greek Pumpkin Pie (Kolokythópita)
- Saffron-Infused Vanilla Bavarois
- Classic Profiteroles
- Pistachio Pavlova with Berries

Yogurt & Granola — 184

Avocado Coconut Pudding
Blueberry Yogurt with Chickpea Topping
Graham Cracker Coriander Yogurt Cups
Strawberry Coconut Yogurt
Blueberry Yogurt Granola Jar
Maple Apple Yogurt Jar
Banana Yogurt Granola Jar
Peach Yogurt Granola Jar
Nut Pomegranate Granola Yogurt Bowl
Orange Yogurt Granola

Snacks — 210

Lemon-Mint Pesto Tartines
Lebanese Dried Apricot Spread
Mouloukhiye Yogurt Dip
Halloumi Spinach Green Pepper Balls
Lentil Dip
Beet Chips
Navy Bean Dip
Tomato Bites
Bocconcini Tomato Mini Tart
Savory Sun-Dried Olive Biscuits
Feta Blueberry Duck Scones

Drinks/Smoothies — 234

Watermelon Rosewater Refresher
Coconut Blueberry Smoothie
Asparagus Blueberry Drink
Avocado Coconut Smoothie
Beet Mango Ginger Smoothie
Kiwi Orange-Flower Smoothie
Green Kale Smoothie
Watermelon Lime Drink
Red Pepper Berry Smoothie
Pear Spinach Smoothie
Sweet Potato Orange Juice
Asparagus Citrus Rosewater
Pumpkin Blueberry Smoothie
Pitaya Smoothie
Mocha Banana Smoothie

Sources — 266

Index — 268

Introduction

It's no secret that the Mediterranean Diet is one of the healthiest in the world. We know this because people who live in the Mediterranean region have less heart disease, lower cholesterol, and lower blood pressure than elsewhere in the world. These health benefits are all thanks to the wholesome, fresh foods that compose their diets, which are usually enhanced with a sprinkle of nuts and seeds! Add up these facts and it's clear why people who live in the Mediterranean boast healthier weights and longer lives.

Now I'm sure you're wondering how this translates into tantalizing dessert recipes. Well, individuals from the Mediterranean often eat dessert; and the health benefits they experience from the overall diet are not swayed by the addition of sweets. This discovery taught me how to treat myself with satisfying desserts, without disrupting my health.

When I became a lifestyle and recipe coach, I avoided making desserts. I focused solely on recipes for breakfast, lunch, and dinner. Desserts simply triggered my fear of overeating something I truly craved. Because I struggled with my weight for years, I felt as though I had no willpower when it came to indulging in calorie-dense treats. It also didn't thrill my clients that I avoided something that was, for many, a satisfying end to a fine meal.

This is where the Mediterranean Diet comes in. After graduating culinary school, I traveled around the Mediterranean, absorbing inspiration from the traditional techniques and classic dishes. When I came back to America, the Mediterranean Diet was not as popular as it is now, and many clients preferred American foods to the Mediterranean ones I introduced to them. So, most my baking focused on calorie-dense, multi-layered desserts that made me feel uncontrollable.

Thankfully, things have changed.

Since then, the Mediterranean Diet has gained traction and worldwide recognition. It occurred to me that Mediterranean desserts involve more than sugar and butter—they're dynamic, bursting with surprising flavors. Desserts used to mean cake, cookies, and pies. Now it means fruit, sauces, and pastries. Instead of restriction, I think about moderation, satisfaction, and sharing. With the Mediterranean mindset, I treat myself often and never feel guilty about it. I don't worry about how desserts affect my waistline because I can trust myself around them.

In retrospect, it all makes sense. The high fiber and protein found in the Mediterranean Diet—fruit, seeds, nuts, and yogurt, among others—were also the main Ingredients in their desserts. It was also the Mediterranean outlook that helped me; I learned that my dissatisfaction wasn't just about the food I ate, but also the way I ate it. I never savored the flavors. I never took time between bites. I never focused on the dessert, only the thought that I had to stop myself. I was never present in my enjoyment. This is a key mindset when it comes to desserts—especially if you're prone to cravings or binging.

After many experiments and lifestyle changes, I've finally found my happy place with desserts. The recipes in this book came from overcoming my fear of desserts. By the time I had written, tested, and selected these recipes, I had officially embraced the Mediterranean approach to desserts. Because of that, these recipes hold a special place in my heart, and they represent the transformation of my inner beliefs.

The recipes you're about to see may surprise you. A few of these desserts may include the amount of butter, eggs, or sugars that you're used to. That's okay—read on to understand how desserts can benefit your health (even the sugary ones)! Whenever a dessert has greater amounts of these Ingredients, just be sure to *eat* like a Mediterranean. That means finding satisfaction in smaller servings than you're used to! Remember, American servings are always far bigger than your appetite.

I also discovered that with some tweaks, many of my recipes could be vegan friendly. Read below if you're looking for those substitutions.

So, if any of what I've said here resonates with you, or if you prefer making healthier options due to the health issues of friends or family members—put those thoughts to rest and discover the health benefits of the Mediterranean approach to desserts!

The Mediterranean Approach

It's well known that Americans don't have the best eating habits. We tend to focus on food as fuel, versus food as an experience. We shove down our meals and run out the door for work, school, practice, or other commitments. I remember as a kid, we never spent more than ten minutes at the table because we were always in a rush.

It's as though meals are a mode of transition in life. We consider meals a transition between one event and another. For example, when I was young, dinner was a transition between homework and dance practice. We never sat at the table to appreciate the food. We sat at the table to eat, energizing us for our next commitment.

This is where our distance from food comes from. We never had the chance to learn the pleasure of food. A meal wasn't—and isn't—about the present moment.

That's where the Mediterranean approach to food comes in. It's all about being present. It's about enjoying the experience of the meal, the company, and the moment.

It almost sounds meditative, and I think it is! It took me awhile to make the switch because being present isn't something that came easy to me. These are a few tips that helped me make the change:

1. While eating, think about the Ingredients in your meal;
2. Wait at least one minute between bites;
3. Ask your family what they think about the food (taste, texture, anything that comes to mind);
4. Think of three things you enjoy about the meal;
5. Stay at the table for at least the same amount of time it took to cook the meal.

Some of these habits you may already put to use! I find these tips really helped me stay focused when experiencing my meal.

So, what does being present have to do with eating desserts? It's all about trusting yourself.

It's about enjoying each bite, each flavor, because if you don't find enjoyment from the dessert, it won't satisfy you. If you're not satisfied, you'll end up binging or restricting yourself later on; which leads to guilt and distrust.

If you trust yourself around desserts, you'll be able to eat one serving when you desire it. You'll notice that it quenches your craving, and it may even lift your mood!

Once you feel in control around desserts, you can learn to incorporate them into your diet. You'll trust yourself around them and the guilt will dissolve.

Another aspect of being present is acknowledging and appreciating the company you have during each meal. Sharing meals with loved ones is a common Mediterranean practice that has many health benefits.

Psychologically speaking, sharing a meal connects us with others, giving us a sense of belonging. It also allows us to reflect on our day, making us feel understood and appreciative.

During these experiences, people tend to eat slower because they talk and listen, which helps our digestive system. Eating at a slower pace gives our stomach time to catch up with the amount eaten, more accurately indicating when you're full.

If you live alone, this may be difficult to incorporate into your lifestyle. However, there are many suggested activities that you can try:

- Host a weekly potluck
- Attend a group cooking class
- Invite friends to a new restaurant
- Host a pizza-making night
- Volunteer at a soup kitchen

Even if you find one day a week for communal eating, you'll still experience health benefits. If you're not a fan of cooking, suggest a potluck or go out. Make sure that whatever you choose, you enjoy the experience. That way you're inclined to make it a habit!

The Mediterranean approach is an organic way of interacting with food; and while it seems simple, it takes time to learn. Be present with your meals and share them with others. Appreciate what's on your plate and attentively enjoy the experience of eating it. Hopefully, this approach will help heal your relationship with food, like it did mine.

Desserts the Mediterranean Way

Mediterranean desserts are quite diverse because the cuisine is influenced by its nine regions: Italy, Spain, Egypt, Greece, Portugal, France, Turkey, Libya, and Morocco! Diversity comes from the influences of these native cuisines that are dependent on the climate and terrain. For example, many coastal cities did not have the proper terrain for livestock, so they relied on seafood instead!

Of course, I was inspired by the Mediterranean region with the recipes within these pages, but I also took a few liberties, such as using maple syrup as a sweetener. I also use fruits that are not traditionally used in Mediterranean dishes but work well in the recipe (think cranberries). Below is a detailed list of Ingredients with an explanation of why they are native to this cuisine, along with Ingredients that can be substituted due to personal preferences, allergies, or other health concerns and restrictions.

Ingredients and Substitutions

Chocolate

Chocolate is common in many Mediterranean recipes (usually a dark variety with more than 70% cocoa), but rather than being used as the main ingredient (chocolate cakes, cookies, brownies) it's used in a limited way. Dark chocolate varieties are also less sweet as they contain less sugar, depending on the percentage of cocoa. The higher the amount of cocoa, the less sugar, and pure cocoa has no sugar at all.

Chocolate as an ingredient is often in the form of chips or a small amount of cocoa powder, which may be diluted with another ingredient, such as coconut cream. By limiting the amount in a recipe, chocolate can still satisfy a sugar craving, but without the sugar rush and sweet-induced headache.

Substitutions

A Mediterranean-inspired cocoa alternative is carob, which is grown on trees. These trees produce leathery pods that contain seeds, which brown as they ripen. A nutty-flavored powder can be created by drying, roasting, and grinding the edible pulp that comes from inside the pods. Carob powder is naturally sweet whereas cocoa powder is bitter. Loaded with fiber, consider carob if you're looking for natural sweetener!

Another option for reducing the amount of sugar in a recipe containing chocolate is to substitute 3 tablespoons of unsweetened cocoa powder and 1 tablespoon of olive oil for every ounce of chocolate. This is a popular and tasty option for vegans!

Chocolate is also used in recipes because it functions as a binder and helps Ingredients blend and stick together. Purées made from hot water and dates, figs, prunes (and even black beans), can make viable and healthier substitutes. In a food processor or blender, combine 3-parts dates, figs, or prunes with 1-part hot water. This purée can substitute for chocolate on a one-to-one ratio! Another option is to use strained prune baby food as a one-to-one substitute. Either way, be sure to adjust the sugar in a recipe for the added sweetness that comes from using fruit. Personally, I love using dates in my dessert bars. It's a fresh take and pulls everything together.

Finally, chocolate chips or chunks add texture to desserts along with the added calories. If texture is your goal, chia seeds are the answer as they not only reduce calories, but also boost protein content. Personally, I'm a big fan and top many of my desserts with a sprinkle of chia seeds.

Another chocolate chip alternative is berries. They taste amazing in desserts and enhance texture, all while adding a bit of extra fiber.

Fruit

Fruit is perhaps the ingredient most associated with Mediterranean desserts (after honey). Sweet fruits, such as berries, pineapple, and melons usually play an integral role in these desserts, but feel free to substitute non-traditional fruits such as apples, bananas, and even cranberries. Fresh or frozen works, but seasonal fruits are best. Just remember that fruit is a great way to add a punch of flavor to baked goods and cut down on the added sugar. Get creative and experiment.

Citrus, lemons, limes, and grapefruits are Mediterranean fruits that add a punch of flavor and brighten baked goods, either as part of the recipe or squeezed fresh over a finished dessert.

Nuts and Seeds

Chocolate, caramel, and whipped cream aren't the only toppings for desserts! Nuts and seeds are great alternatives. There is no greater way to add texture to a dish—and a nutritious one at that. Nuts are high in protein, manganese, magnesium, and vitamin E. Seeds contain protein, omega 6, manganese, fiber. Both are healthy sources of fat.

When it comes to nuts and seeds, there are so many options—they can be used in a recipe, or sprinkled over the finished dish, they can be used raw or toasted, and chopped or whole. There is also an amazing number of varieties, such as flax, chia, peanut, pumpkin, almond, pecan, and pistachio.

Olive Oil

Olive oil is the pillar of the Mediterranean Diet, and it also plays a big part in dessert making. Swap out butter for olive oil to reap its health benefits that range from lowering blood pressure, promoting heart health, and reducing inflammation, to improving brain function; plus it's packed with antioxidants. Always choose the extra-virgin variety as it is the least processed and boasts the most health benefits. Also, taste before you buy, if possible. Some have a very neutral taste, while others can lean into the fruity or pungent spectrum. Use the one best suited to your recipe.

Fun fact: When the entire world used butter for cooking, they looked down upon the Mediterranean regions for using olive oil instead. Now we know better!

Butter

Even though olive oil is the healthy fat of choice when it comes to Mediterranean food, butter is often chosen when making some baked goods, but if you want a healthier alternative, consider the following options.

Olive oil: You can always swap out equal amounts of butter for olive oil; just make sure you choose one with a taste that matches your recipe.

Avocado: Loaded with vitamins and healthy plant-based fat, avocados are the epitome of Mediterranean food. Toss aside the skin and pop the avocado flesh into a blender to create the perfect creamy and smooth butter replacement. It's even a perfect one-to-one swap.

Beans: Yes, beans! Beans are a favorite in the Mediterranean community and used in many recipes. Beans are loaded with fiber, protein, iron, and vitamin B. They can also transform a dessert into a healthy oasis. Simply soak and cook the beans, drain, and purée in a food processor or blender. Like avocados, simply swap at a one-to-one ratio with butter. If you're wondering which type of beans to use, think color—white in light-colored recipes and black beans for chocolate desserts.

Eggs

Eggs bind Ingredients and add moisture to desserts. Unfortunately, like milk products, some people are allergic, and they are not available to vegans either! But have no fear, as there are always alternatives.

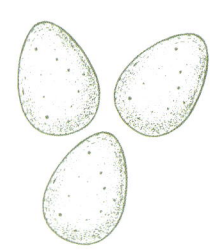

Unsweetened applesauce: This swap offers the same benefits in a recipe as eggs but may make your baking even moister. Swap ¼ cup of applesauce for one whole egg. Not to worry, you won't taste any apple in the finished product.

Banana: Replace a whole egg with ¼ cup of mashed banana. Unlike the applesauce, bananas will add a tinge of sweetness to a recipe, so adjust the sugar.

Silken tofu: Like eggs, tofu adds protein to your diet and keeps you feeling full. This is a "heavier" option, which means it works better in dense cakes, muffins, or pies. Be aware that tofu doesn't brown, so you'll need to test doneness with a toothpick and not rely on color. Swap out ¼ cup of puréed tofu for one whole egg. If the tofu seems too thick, thin with a bit of water.

If a recipe calls for egg whites instead of a whole egg, I suggest cutting the above amounts in half. For example, instead of ¼ cup mashed bananas, use ⅛ of a cup or 2 tablespoons!

Dairy

Heavy cream is high in fat and calories, but it also has health benefits if eaten in moderation; for example, a dollop topping a simple bowl of fresh fruit. It's also high in calcium, and vitamins A, E, D, and K. The fat in cream also helps the body absorb certain vitamins (like D). When choosing any dairy product, it's tempting to choose a low- or fat-free variety, but before you consider those options, just know they contain added sugar and sometimes salt to make up for sacrificing the fat and flavor. Low-fat milk works as an option to be poured on your cereal, but a dollop of whipped cream on a dessert has no peer. When eaten in moderation, heavy cream is a well-deserved and healthy treat.

Lactose Intolerant/Vegan Alternatives

For whipping cream: Mix equal parts of silken tofu and soy milk in a blender or food processor, and beat until thick and fluffy. For extra flavor, add vanilla extract to taste.

For heavy cream used *in* recipes: Combine 2-parts soymilk with 1-part olive oil and mix well. It will be thinner than heavy cream, but it works great.

Dairy heavy cream alternative:* If you're a milk drinker but choose not to use heavy cream in recipes, try this lower-calorie alternative that's high in protein.

Combine equal parts whole milk with plain Greek yogurt and whisk until well combined and smooth.

*Remember, this is not a whipping cream.

Sweeteners

Too much sugar is bad for us—this is a known fact; but like all things in life, moderation is key. It's also important to remember that it isn't only desserts that add to our sugar intake. Sodas, fast foods, and processed foods are loaded with the stuff—check the labels. Put simply, sugar is not the enemy if it's eaten in moderation.

If you are interested in reducing your sugar intake for health reasons, consider swapping sugar for puréed dates! Combine ¾ cup of dates with ¼ cup of hot water in a food processor or blender. This purée will replace 1 cup of sugar!

I only suggest avoiding sugar if you have a health concern. But you can limit sugar in many ways, such as choosing low-sugar foods and swapping processed for whole foods!

Why Do We Get Cravings?

While the Mediterranean approach to food helped heal my distrust around desserts, I've discovered it's also important to understand where this distrust comes from. Why did I feel uncomfortable around desserts in the first place? Why was I inclined to binge instead of enjoy? Why did my cravings feel endless?

Below I discuss the differences between hunger and cravings, hoping it better helps you understand your body's cues and your associations with dessert—and food in general.

Cravings versus Hunger

I'm sure you've experienced cravings before. Most people have experienced at least one craving before, whether it's for a specific food or a type of food.

It's important to differentiate cravings and hunger. Cravings are a desire, while hunger is your body signalling you need more fuel. Sometimes these two can be confused; however, there are some telling differences.

1. Eating rids hunger, but does not always rid a craving;
2. Hunger will not go away until you eat, while cravings eventually go away on their own;
3. Hunger can cause stomach pain and headaches, cravings do not.

Remember, if you feel hungry, your body is communicating that it needs energy. Ignoring hunger is not healthy and can lead to physical and emotional damage, including disordered eating and permanent digestive issues. Simply, not eating when you're hungry will not benefit your diet and can lead to health concerns.

Physical Causes

1. SLEEP
Not getting enough sleep can create cravings. This is because hormones rely on your sleep-cycles (circadian rhythm) to regulate. Without proper sleep, your body's hormones are not regulated, leading to intense cravings. Essentially, if you're awake when you should be sleeping, your body creates hormones to help you maintain energy instead of hormones for sleep. To avoid this, reduce screen time before bed and avoid using lights after the sun has set. This boosts your circadian rhythm and reduces unwanted cravings.

2. PROTEIN AND FIBER
A lack of nutrients can also cause cravings. Your body needs protein and fiber to feel full. If you're not getting enough of these nutrients, your body will still think its hungry—even if you've eaten more than your daily amount of calories. Short story? Get your daily intake of protein and fiber so your body feels satisfied.

3. WATER
I'm sure you've heard about the 8 cups of water a day rule. While repeating it may make you role your eyes, it's worth mentioning here. If you're dehydrated, your body can increase cravings. Similar to not getting enough protein and fiber, your body needs water to feel satisfied.

4. EXERCISE
I know; this is another one you're tired of hearing about. However, did you know that regular exercise can decrease your cravings? You don't need to hit the gym every day, even a nightly walk can reduce your food-related urges. Lots of walking is quite common in the Mediterranean and is encouraged for the countless health benefits. If walking doesn't interest you, try swimming, yoga, or dancing. These require more mental engagement compared to walking and won't bore you. You can also set goals with friends or family, holding each other accountable! That's how I started my yoga journey.

5. FREQUENCY

If you satisfy your cravings, you're likely to crave that item more frequently and more intensely. If you're able to resist your cravings, over time you'll crave them less. This is something that takes strong self-control and self-trust. If you can't resist a craving, that's okay. Start with lessening the frequency you eat it and how much you eat. Avoid going on "free" months, such as chocolate-free January. This creates an all or nothing mindset, which usually ends with intense cravings, creating guilt. Nothing should be entirely off-limits unless you have a health concern or an allergy.

6. HORMONES

Shout out to my fellow menstruators; it is extremely common for hormones to cause cravings. During PMS (Premenstrual Syndrome), estrogen and progesterone shifts can create cravings for carb-rich foods. It should be noted that there are other hormonal causes of cravings, including pregnancy, menopause, medications, and imbalances in leptin and ghrelin. These two hormones control your feelings related to hunger and fullness. While these causes are difficult to ignore, try eating protein- and fiber-rich foods before succumbing to your craving. Your body may just need nourishment. If the craving persists, fulfill it, in moderation.

Psychological Causes

1. STRESS

Stress eating is a fairly common behavior. When you're stressed the hormone cortisol is released, which can cause intense cravings. An obvious answer is to avoid stress, but depending on your situation, that may not be an option. If stress is inevitable for you, remember to fuel yourself with the appropriate foods and hydrate. Similar to hormones, if you're still craving something, enjoy a small amount. If you find your stress causes binging, please consult your doctor.

2. CHARACTER

People who identify as impulsive are more likely to experience cravings. In terms of personality, those with adventurous, impulsive, or addictive traits are connected with cravings. This is most likely due to a lack of control. Read the following section for tips that will prevent impulsive eating behaviours.

3. ENVIRONMENT

When you go to a café for coffee, do the donuts pique your interest? When you're at the movies, do you automatically order popcorn? If you answered yes, you're not alone. Environment has a strong impact on our cravings. Try to notice when this happens for you and check in with your hunger levels before ordering.

4. MENTAL ILLNESS

Those plagued with negative emotions can experience intense cravings. This is because those with depression have lower levels of serotonin. This is a neurotransmitter which regulates mood. Some foods, especially those rich in carbs, lift serotonin levels, which helps those with the mental illness feel happier. In a way, it's a form of self-medicating and is not recommended as treatment. If you experience mental illness, consult your doctor and find yourself a therapist you feel comfortable around.

Gaining Control

While there are many causes of cravings, there's good news. You can gain control over your cravings with a four-step method. While it may take time (and it's okay if it does), it's important to remember that any progress is better than none. If you satisfy your craving, don't be hard on yourself. I cater to my cravings sometimes—ensuring it's only one serving and by remaining present.

The first step is acknowledging your cravings. When you start to crave something, notice it. Ask yourself why you're craving this. Look back on the causes and try to identify which one resonates with you. Are you feeling down? Is it your time of month? Are you dehydrated or lacking nutrients? Check in with yourself. If it's something you can change, like eating fiber-rich foods, swap your craving for that.

The next step will take time; ensure you are giving your body what it needs. Keep water near you at all times. If you hate water, add some fruit or lemon juice. My go-to is a few lemon slices with a sprig of rosemary. Get in your daily protein and fiber requirements. High-protein foods include eggs, nuts, meat, oats, cheese, broccoli, lentils, and fish. High-fiber foods include pears, apples, raspberries (also good in water!), avocados, kidney beans, chickpeas, oats, and popcorn!

Learning these behaviours will take time. Be patient and allow yourself to make mistakes.

The third step is Mediterranean inspired. Be mindful about your food choices. This is the most difficult step, but it will offer the most help. Plan your foods around the causes of your cravings. Enrich your diet with protein, fiber, and other nutrients. Choose your foods wisely. Stay present with your cravings and eat in moderation. If your sweet tooth is acting up, eat a bite of chocolate and wait it out. Most likely, if you allow yourself to enjoy that bite, your craving will fade away. The more present you are when you eat, the more likely your brain will acknowledge the intake of food, reducing cravings.

The final step is to discuss your cravings with your doctor. If you're not getting enough sleep or your hormones are not regulated, your doctor can help you find solutions. Give steps one through three time, but if you're still not satisfied, there may be an underlying health concern. As briefly mentioned above, medications can affect your cravings. If this is the case, your doctor may offer alternatives.

At the end of the day, don't beat yourself up if you "give in" to your temptations. Cravings are normal and common. Just remember to portion the foods you eat to satisfy your cravings. Don't feel guilty. Don't feel bad. Following through with a craving occasionally won't destroy your health and won't reverse your progress.

Do Desserts Have Health Benefits?

Now that we've discussed cravings, control, and mindful eating, it's time to cover the health benefits of desserts. I bet you're thinking, *"Health benefits of desserts? What is she talking about?!"*

I promise I'm not making it up! There is scientific proof that desserts are good for you—in moderation. Once you trust yourself around desserts, you can actually use them to benefit your health.

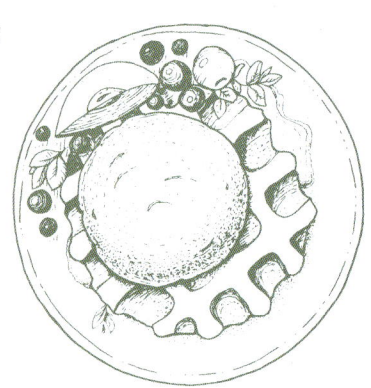

This may surprise you, but eating sweet breakfasts, like pancakes with maple syrup, can prevent cravings throughout the day. In a study, 100 adults ate a 600-calorie breakfast, including multiple sweets, such as a cookie, donut, and cake. Another 100 adults ate a 300-calorie breakfast loaded with nutrients, including tuna, egg whites, and cheese.

Those on the "healthy" breakfast reported more cravings than those who began their morning with sweets. Researchers believe this is because our bodies need a lot of calories to start the day. It helps keep us energized for the entire day (only if you eat throughout the day as well).

Again, this is suggested in moderation. If you're going to eat pancakes with maple syrup every day, stick to a pancake or two, while incorporating fruits and Greek yogurt.

Another fun benefit of dessert? Chocolate lowers blood pressure. Yes, you read that right! Just a few nibbles of chocolate can lower your blood pressure. It's because of the flavonoids in the cocoa. Rich in antioxidants and anti-inflammatory benefits, flavonoids lower blood pressure. Always go for dark chocolate over milk chocolate, as it has more cocoa and therefore more flavonoids.

That's not the only benefit of cocoa. It also raises your levels of serotonin, which boosts your mood. Small portions of chocolate simply make you happier!

If you savor each bite when you eat dessert, you'll feel satisfied sooner. This means that if you stay mindful while eating dessert, you're better able to gauge when to stop. You'll be more satisfied with one serving if you're actively paying attention to the dish. If you're distracted, it will take much longer and much more for you to experience satisfaction.

In a study, it was found that those who paid attention to the number of bites they ate, were satisfied sooner than those who did not count their bites. It even helped the participants lose weight! Obviously, mindful eating is a good habit to get into with all foods, but it's particularly important with desserts because it's easier to lose control around them.

Have you ever been told you can't do something and then you do it 'just because?' This is a common issue with desserts; we tell ourselves "no" and end up binging. Essentially, it's worse to restrict yourself than to allow yourself a few bites. Allowing yourself to eat dessert, in reasonable portions, helps you satisfy your cravings and move on with your day. A helpful tip is to cut a slice or put aside an amount and remove the rest of the dessert. This helps you commit to your portion and rid your craving. Who would have thought desserts could relieve your cravings?

Heart disease is one of the leading causes of death in America, and while overeating desserts can contribute to this, portioning desserts can prevent strokes! Dark chocolate is good for you. It really is, and as such, it has been proven to reduce your risk of strokes. In a study, those who ate a few bites of dark chocolate a day were significantly less likely to experience strokes.

Another benefit of certain desserts is that they act as an aphrodisiac. Having trouble getting in the mood? Have a slice of pumpkin pie after dinner! The seeds contain zinc, which increases testosterone. A study proved that just the smell of pumpkin pie could increase your libido. This study also found that eating pumpkin pie increased blood flow in men, while lowering anxiety in both men and women. Another study discovered that participants who ate a small amount of chocolate each day engaged in more sexual activity.

Now, I'm not saying to eat a bunch of desserts to put yourself in the mood or to fuel your entire day; what I'm saying is that desserts are not evil. Foods are not good or bad; every food in moderation has some benefits, including desserts. It's important to enjoy yourself occasionally, and a treat can do just that.

Mediterranean Desserts

As you can imagine, the Mediterranean is bursting with creative and imaginative desserts—whether completely original or a variation of what's tried and true.

When you read through these recipes, remember that desserts are meant to be fun. Many originate from celebrations. When you try these recipes, enjoy the taste, experience the flavor, and be present.

You don't have to stop your Mediterranean education with these recipes, you can also learn from their cultural practices. Share your sweets with loved ones. Drop them off as a surprise or bake them in preparation of a celebration. Stay present when you eat these desserts. Allow yourself to enjoy the moment and don't rush. Think about the effort you put into making these treats as you take each bite.

Moderation is key, but so is enjoyment.

The following collection of Mediterranean-inspired desserts is a personal thanks from me to you. Thank you for believing in my food journey. Thank you for trusting my recipes. Thank you for allowing me to share my experience with you and hopefully you learned something—about desserts, cravings, or even yourself.

Main Desserts

Honey Pecan Mascarpone Cups

Makes 4–6 cups

PREP TIME: 10 minutes • **COOK TIME:** 0 • **TOTAL TIME:** 2 hours 10 minutes
Level 2: Easy

No one will ever guess that this masterpiece of a dessert comes together in less than 15 minutes. Flavored with vanilla extract, honey, and crushed pecans, mascarpone cups get a delicious upgrade. It's versatile enough to be smeared on toasted bread or crackers, or served atop fresh fruit as an afternoon delight, paired with tea.

INGREDIENTS

- 1 cup mascarpone cheese
- ¾ cup pecans, crushed, divided
- 3 tablespoons honey, divided
- 1 tablespoon lemon zest
- 1½ teaspoons vanilla extract

INSTRUCTIONS

1. Combine the mascarpone cheese, ½ cup of pecans, 2 tablespoons of honey, lemon zest, and vanilla extract in a bowl, mixing well.

2. Spoon the mixture into 4–6 dessert dishes, cover with plastic wrap, and chill for 2–3 hours, or until set.

3. Top each with the remaining ¼ cup of pecans and a drizzle of the remaining 1 tablespoon of honey before serving. Refrigerate leftovers in an airtight container for up to 3 days.

NUTRITION · PER ONE SERVING

- Calories **287 (14%)**
- Total Fat **25.84 g (47%)**
  - Saturated Fat **11.712 g**
  - Polyunsaturated Fat **2.236 g**
  - Monounsaturated Fat **8.9 g**
  - *Trans* Fat **0.47g**
- Cholesterol **29.43 mg**
- Sodium **143 mg (9%)**
- Total Carbohydrate: **12.85 g (5%)**
  - Dietary Fiber: **1.3 g (5%)**
  - Total Sugars: **10.91 g**
- Protein: **3.49 g (7%)**
- Vitamin A **516 mcg (21%)**
- Vitamin C **2.8 mcg (4%)**
- Vitamin D **16 mcg (3%)**
- Potassium **158 mg (2%)**
- Calcium **60.12 mg (8%)**
- Iron **0.41 mg (3%)**

Banana Pistachio Oatmeal Cookies

Makes 16 cookies

PREP TIME: 12 minutes • **COOK TIME:** 14 minutes • **TOTAL TIME:** 26 minutes
Level 2: Easy

These Banana Pistachio Oatmeal Cookies—made with only seven ingredients—are the easiest you'll ever make—and the healthiest! Loaded with antioxidants, potassium, and fiber, this dessert will leave you feeling your best, all while satisfying your sweet tooth.

INGREDIENTS

- 2 cups old-fashioned rolled oats (not quick oats)
- 3 medium ripe bananas, mashed
- ½ cup cashew butter
- ⅓ cup semi-sweet chocolate chips
- ⅓ cup shelled pistachios, chopped
- ⅓ cup dried cherries, coarsely chopped
- ⅓ cup coconut, shredded

INSTRUCTIONS

1. Preheat oven to 325°F and line a cookie sheet with parchment paper.

2. Combine oats, mashed bananas, and cashew butter in a large bowl, mixing well.

3. Add the chocolate chips, pistachios, dried cherries, and shredded coconut, and stir to combine.

4. Drop tablespoon-sized scoops of batter 1½-inch apart on the prepared cookie sheet and slightly flatten with a fork.

5. Bake for 12–14 minutes, until cookies start to brown around the edges.

6. Cool cookies on the pan for 5 minutes, then transfer to a wire rack to cool completely.

7. Serve and enjoy! Refrigerate leftovers in an airtight container for up to 3 days.

NUTRITION · PER ONE SERVING

Calories **199 (9%)**
Total Fat **9.1 g (19%)**
    Saturated Fat **4.688 g**
    Polyunsaturated Fat **1.091 g**
    Monounsaturated Fat **2.58 g**
    Trans Fat **0.233 g**
Cholesterol **15 mg**
Sodium **56 mg (4%)**
Total Carbohydrate: **26.68 g (11%)**
    Dietary Fiber: **3.2 g (13%)**
    Total Sugars: **9.02 g**

Protein: **4.34 g (8%)**
Vitamin A **295 mcg (13%)**
Vitamin C **2.7 mcg (4%)**
Vitamin D **4 mcg (1%)**
Potassium **223 mg (5%)**
Calcium **18 mg (2%)**
Iron **1.27 mg (7%)**

Chocolate Apricot Pudding

Makes 4 servings

PREP TIME: 15 minutes • **COOK TIME:** 0 • **TOTAL TIME:** 2 hours 15 minutes
Level 1: Very Easy

Unlike traditional puddings, this one is free of eggs and dairy, and instead uses a secret ingredient—chia seeds. Chia seeds not only make this pudding vegan-friendly, they also boast fiber and protein, while thickening the pudding to the classic velvety consistency everyone loves.

INGREDIENTS

- ¾ cup chia seeds
- ¼ cup unsweetened cocoa powder
- 3 tablespoons stevia
- 2½ cups almond milk
- 1 teaspoon vanilla extract
- ¾ cup dried apricots, finely chopped and divided

INSTRUCTIONS

1. Whisk together the chia seeds, cocoa powder, and stevia in a large bowl.

2. Add the almond milk and vanilla extract, whisking until free of lumps. Once combined, stir in ½ cup of chopped apricots.

3. Cover the bowl with plastic wrap and refrigerate for 2 hours or overnight, until set.

4. To serve, stir the pudding and spoon into 4 serving dishes. Top each dish with the remaining ¼ cup of chopped apricots or any other fruit of your preference.

NUTRITION • PER ONE SERVING

Calories **362 (17%)**	Protein: **13.54 g (25%)**
Total Fat **18.86 g (25%)**	Vitamin A **2155 mcg (92%)**
Saturated Fat **4.684 g**	Vitamin C **2.1 mg (3%)**
Polyunsaturated Fat **10.402 g**	Vitamin D **3 mcg (1%)**
Monounsaturated Fat **2.496 g**	Potassium **786 mg (17%)**
Trans Fat **0.06 g**	Calcium **456 mg (46%)**
Cholesterol **15 mg**	Iron **5.1 mg (28%)**
Sodium **75 mg (5%)**	
Total Carbohydrate: **51.42 g (21%)**	
Dietary Fiber: **17.1 g (69%)**	
Total Sugars: **7.93 g**	

Four Ingredient Tahini Nut Fudge

Makes 8 servings

PREP TIME: 10 minutes • **COOK TIME:** 11 minutes • **TOTAL TIME:** 3 hours 21 minutes
Level 2: Easy

No dessert selection is complete without fudge. Fudge is simplicity at its best. Made with only four Ingredients, the most challenging part about making this treat is the 3 hours you'll need to wait for it to set! I guarantee that after one bite of this creamy velvety confection, you'll forget all about the wait as you reach for seconds.

INGREDIENTS

½ cup shelled pistachios, chopped

½ cup walnuts, chopped

½ cup honey

1 cup tahini

INSTRUCTIONS

1. Preheat oven to 350°F and line both an 8-×-8-inch pan and a cookie sheet with parchment paper.

2. Arrange the pistachios and walnuts in a single layer on the prepared cookie sheet and bake for 8 minutes, or until the pistachios are golden. Remove from oven and allow to cool for 5 minutes.

3. Heat the honey in a saucepan set over high heat for 2–3 minutes, until it boils, then remove from heat.

4. Add the tahini and whisk until smooth, but stiff. Stir in the pistachios and walnuts.

5. Spread the soft fudge in an even layer on the prepared pan.

6. Allow fudge to set for 3 hours.

7. Cut into 8 squares before serving. Refrigerate leftovers in an airtight container for up to 3 days.

NUTRITION · PER ONE SERVING

Calories **319 (15%)**

Total Fat **22.88 g (47%)**
  Saturated Fat **2.992 g**
  Polyunsaturated Fat **10.484 g**
  Monounsaturated Fat **28.368 g**
  Trans Fat **0 g**

Cholesterol **0 mg**

Sodium **36 mg (2%)**

Total Carbohydrate: **26.62 g (11%)**
  Dietary Fiber: **4 g (16%)**
  Total Sugars: **0.13 g**

Protein: **7.48 g (14%)**

Vitamin A **53 mcg (2%)**

Vitamin C **0.6 mcg (1%)**

Vitamin D **0 mcg**

Potassium **236 mg (5%)**

Calcium **142 mg (14%)**

Iron **3.22 mg (18%)**

Chocolate Apricot Truffles

Makes 12 truffles

PREP TIME: 30 minutes • **COOK TIME:** 2 minutes • **TOTAL TIME:** 32 minutes

Level 2: Easy

Chocolate and apricots make for a stellar pairing, and if you add almonds and cinnamon, you've got a truly mouth-watering combination. In true Mediterranean fashion, this dreamy dessert is loaded with nutrients, including vitamin A and iron! I promise that these Chocolate Apricot Truffles are unlike anything you've ever tasted.

INGREDIENTS

- 1 cup dried apricots
- ½ cup blanched cashews
- ¾ cup boiling water
- 1 teaspoon cinnamon
- ¼ cup dark chocolate, chopped

INSTRUCTIONS

1. Line a cookie sheet with parchment paper.

2. Place the apricots and cashews in a heat-safe bowl and cover with the boiling water, stir and allow to soak for 5 minutes, then drain.

3. Place the apricots and cashews into a food processor. Add cinnamon and blend, until the mixture forms a thick paste.

4. Using a tablespoon, scoop up the mixture and roll into balls. Place them on the cookie sheet, 1-inch apart.

5. Place the dark chocolate into a heat-safe bowl and microwave for 30 seconds, then stir. Microwave for 10 more seconds and stir. Continue in 10 second intervals, stirring in between until the chocolate is melted, around 1 minute total. Once completely melted, remove chocolate from the microwave.

6. Using a fork, dip each truffle into the chocolate, making sure each one is thoroughly coated in chocolate and the excess has dripped off before returning truffles to the cookie sheet.

7. Place the cookie sheet into the fridge. Do not disturb the truffles until the chocolate sets, around 5 minutes.

8. Serve once truffles cool completely. Refrigerate leftovers in an airtight container for up to 3 days.

NUTRITION • PER ONE SERVING

Calories **109 (5%)**
Total Fat **7.15 g (15%)**
   Saturated Fat **2.022 g**
   Polyunsaturated Fat **1.477 g**
   Monounsaturated Fat **3.299 g**
   Trans Fat **0 g**
Cholesterol **0 mg**
Sodium **34 mg (2%)**
Total Carbohydrate: **10.97 g (4%)**
   Dietary Fiber: **1.7 g (7%)**
   Total Sugars: **6.79 g**

Protein: **2.06 g (4%)**
Vitamin A **391 mcg (17%)**
Vitamin C **0.1 mcg**
Vitamin D **0 mcg**
Potassium **197 mg (4%)**
Calcium **19 mg (2%)**
Iron **1.31 mg (7%)**

Roasted Apricots

Makes 6 servings

PREP TIME: 15 minutes • **COOK TIME:** 12 minutes • **TOTAL TIME:** 27 minutes
Level 2: Easy

Sometimes the simplest Ingredients make the tastiest desserts, and this recipe is no exception. As the apricots roast, they exude a lovely syrup, adding a luscious texture and flavor to this dish. Serve these Roasted Apricots on a slice of cake or over ice cream for a marvelous pairing. Just wait for your dinner guests to clear their plates!

INGREDIENTS

6 fresh apricots, washed, halved, and pitted

3 tablespoons brown sugar

2 tablespoons butter, room temperature

1 teaspoon vanilla extract

1 teaspoon ground cinnamon

½ teaspoon nutmeg

¼ teaspoon ground cloves

INSTRUCTIONS

1. Preheat oven to 375°F and line a cookie sheet with parchment paper.

2. Place apricot halves cut side up on the prepared cookie sheet and set aside.

3. Combine sugar, butter, vanilla extract, cinnamon, nutmeg, and cloves in a bowl, mixing well.

4. Place an equal amount of the spiced butter mixture into the center of each apricot half.

5. Bake the apricots for 12 minutes, until golden.

6. Remove from oven and allow the apricots to rest for 10–15 minutes.

7. Serve once cooled. Refrigerate leftovers in an airtight container for up to 3 days.

NUTRITION · PER ONE SERVING

Calories **71 (3%)**
Total Fat **4.06 g (8%)**
  Saturated Fat **2.493 g**
  Polyunsaturated Fat **0.175 g**
  Monounsaturated Fat **1.063 g**
  Trans Fat **0.155 g**
Cholesterol **10 mg**
Sodium **31 mg (2%)**
Total Carbohydrate: **8.47 g (3%)**
  Dietary Fiber: **1 g (4%)**
Total Sugars: **7.25 g**

Protein: **0.56 g (1%)**
Vitamin A **794 mcg (34%)**
Vitamin C **3.5 mcg (5%)**
Vitamin D **3 mcg (1%)**
Potassium **96 mg (2%)**
Calcium **11 mg (1%)**
Iron **0.19 mg (1%)**

Chocolate Hummus

Makes 4 servings

PREP TIME: 11 minutes • **COOK TIME:** 0 • **TOTAL TIME:** 11 minutes
Level 2: Easy

Hummus isn't just an appetizer ... it can be a dessert too! This Chocolate Hummus is the perfect light dessert, bringing any meal to a satisfying close. It's creamy and fluffy, and best served with pita or cinnamon-sugar tortilla chips. As with other Mediterranean desserts, this hummus is a rich source of vitamins and minerals, improving digestion and aiding in weight management.

INGREDIENTS

1 (15-oz.) can garbanzo beans, rinsed and drained

¼ cup cocoa powder

4 tablespoons maple syrup

1 teaspoon cinnamon

1 teaspoon vanilla extract

Zest of 1 lemon

1–2 tablespoons water

INSTRUCTIONS

1. Combine garbanzo beans, cocoa powder, maple syrup, cinnamon, vanilla extract, and lemon zest in a blender or food processor and purée until slightly smooth.

2. Add the water in one tablespoon at a time and continue to purée until the hummus reaches the desired consistency.

3. Spoon into a serving dish and serve! Refrigerate leftovers in an airtight container for up to 3 days.

NUTRITION · PER ONE SERVING

Calories **220 (10%)**
Total Fat **4.2 g (4.5%)**
   Saturated Fat **0.54 g (3%)**
   Polyunsaturated Fat **1.06 g**
   Monounsaturated Fat **0.76 g**
   Trans Fat **0 g**
Cholesterol **0 mg**
Sodium **267 mg (18%)**
Total Carbohydrate: **42.69 g (17%)**
   Dietary Fiber: **8.9 g (36%)**
   Total Sugars: **17.33 g**

Protein: **8.65 g (16%)**
Vitamin A **27 mcg (1%)**
Vitamin C **4.8 mcg (6%)**
Vitamin D **0 mcg**
Potassium **331 mg (7%)**
Calcium **82 mg (8%)**
Iron **2.09 mg (12%)**

Pistachio Ice Cream

Makes 6 servings

PREP TIME: 30 minutes • **COOK TIME:** 0 • **TOTAL TIME:** 7 hours 30 minutes
Level 1: Very Easy

Crafted with both roasted pistachios and pistachio butter, this dairy-free ice cream is absolutely irresistible, and I assure you, one scoop will never be enough! So eat up, because this is one dessert that keeps your blood sugar, cholesterol, and blood pressure in check.

INGREDIENTS

2 cups unsweetened almond milk

½ cup pistachio butter

⅓ cup granulated sugar

1 teaspoon vanilla extract

¼ teaspoon salt

¾ cup unsalted pistachios, roasted and chopped

INSTRUCTIONS

1. Whisk together all Ingredients together in a bowl, except pistachio nuts. Blend well.*

2. Transfer mixture to an airtight freezer-safe container with a lid, cover, and freeze for two hours.

3. Remove from freezer and stir again. Refreeze mixture for another two hours.

4. Uncover mixture and add the chopped pistachios, stirring one last time. Cover and return to freezer for another 3–4 hours, or until firm.

5. Once desired consistency is reached, serve in small dessert bowls.

NOTE: *If using an ice cream maker: Place blended mixture in ice cream maker and follow manufacturer's directions.

NUTRITION · PER ONE SERVING

Calories **218 (10%)**
Total Fat **14.21 g (29%)**
  Saturated Fat **2.926 g**
  Polyunsaturated Fat **3.636 g**
  Monounsaturated Fat **6.744 g**
  Trans Fat **0 g**
Cholesterol **8 mg**
Sodium **133 mg (9%)**
Total Carbohydrate: **16.8 g (7%)**
  Dietary Fiber: **2.6 g (10%)**
Total Sugars: **11.55 g**

Protein: **7.86 g (14%)**
Vitamin A **214 mcg (9%)**
Vitamin C **1 mcg (1%)**
Vitamin D **2 mcg**
Potassium **368 mg (8%)**
Calcium **119 mg (12%)**
Iron **1.05 mg (6%)**

Lemon Thyme Coconut Ice Cream

Makes 5 servings

PREP TIME: 35 minutes • **COOK TIME:** 5 minutes • **TOTAL TIME:** 8 hours 10 minutes
Level 2: Easy

Ice cream is usually sweet, but sometimes the combination of sweet and savory is quite literally the best of both worlds. The lemon and thyme meld together beautifully, producing a unique flavor that everyone will love. Boasting vitamin C and soluble fiber, you'll feel good treating yourself with this dessert.

INGREDIENTS

- 1½ cups canned coconut milk
- ½ cup coconut cream
- ½ cup maple syrup
- 1 sprig of fresh thyme
- Zest of 1 lemon
- ¼ teaspoon sea salt
- 1 tablespoon lemon juice
- 1½ teaspoons vanilla extract

INSTRUCTIONS

1. Combine coconut milk, coconut cream, maple syrup, thyme, lemon zest, and salt in a medium saucepan set over medium-high heat. Stir constantly for 3–5 minutes, until it just begins to boil. Remove from heat and cover.

2. Cool mixture completely (approximately 1½ hours).*

3. Once cool, strain mixture through a fine-mesh sieve into an airtight freezer-safe bowl with a lid.

4. Stir in the lemon juice and vanilla extract, cover, and freeze for two hours.

5. Remove from freezer and stir again. Refreeze mixture for another two hours and stir again before refreezing for an additional two hours.

6. Once desired consistency is reached, serve in small dessert bowls.

NOTE: *If using an ice cream maker: Place mixture in ice cream maker and follow manufacturer's directions. Churn the Lemon Thyme Coconut Ice Cream base into the machine after you have mixed all of the Ingredients.

NUTRITION · PER ONE SERVING

Calories **328 (15%)**
Total Fat **19.35 g (40%)**
   Saturated Fat **17.414 g**
   Polyunsaturated Fat **0.216 g**
   Monounsaturated Fat **0.821 g**
   Trans Fat **0 g**
Cholesterol **0 mg**
Sodium **140 mg (9%)**
Total Carbohydrate: **39.92 g (16%)**
   Dietary Fiber: **0.1 g (1%)**
   Total Sugars: **34.77 g**

Protein: **1.8 g (3%)**
Vitamin A **24 mcg (24%)**
Vitamin C **6.3 mcg (8%)**
Vitamin D **0 mcg**
Potassium **264 mg (6%)**
Calcium **48 mg (5%)**
Iron **2.41 mg (13%)**

Roasted Fruit Medley

Makes 6 servings

PREP TIME: 30 minutes • **COOK TIME:** 12 minutes • **TOTAL TIME:** 42 minutes
Level 2: Easy

Just as roasting brings out the best flavors in vegetables, roasting fruit allows their natural sugars to ooze out and caramelize into a nutty, toasty, buttery syrup, creating a mouth-watering sauce. If you really want to wow your family, serve this delightful Roasted Fruit Medley over ice cream or gelato!

INGREDIENTS

3 apricots, washed, pitted, and quartered

3 cactus pears, washed, stem and blossom ends trimmed, and quartered

12 small fresh figs, washed and halved

¼ cup butter, room temperature

3 tablespoons brown sugar

3 tablespoons honey

1 teaspoon vanilla extract

1 teaspoon ground cinnamon

½ teaspoon nutmeg

INSTRUCTIONS

1. Preheat oven to 375°F and line a cookie sheet with parchment paper.

2. Dry fruit, place all pieces cut side up onto the prepared cookie sheet, and set aside.

3. Combine butter, sugar, honey, vanilla extract, cinnamon, and nutmeg in a bowl, mixing well.

4. Spread butter mixture onto the fleshy side of each piece of fruit and roast in the oven for 12 minutes.

5. Remove from oven and allow roasted fruit to rest for 10–15 minutes.

6. Serve warm or at room temperature. Refrigerate leftovers in an airtight container for up to 3 days.

NUTRITION · PER ONE SERVING

Calories **239 (11%)**
Total Fat **8.18 g (17%)**
   Saturated Fat **4.984 g**
   Polyunsaturated Fat **0.501 g**
   Monounsaturated Fat **2.154 g**
   Trans Fat **0.31 g**
Cholesterol **20 mg**
Sodium **65 mg (4%)**
Total Carbohydrate: **44.44 g (18%)**
   Dietary Fiber: **5.7 g (23%)**
   Total Sugars: **36.4 g**

Protein: **1.31 g (2%)**
Vitamin A **711 mcg (30%)**
Vitamin C **7.3 mcg (10%)**
Vitamin D **6 mcg (1%)**
Potassium **351 mg (7%)**
Calcium **50 mg (5%)**
Iron **0.64 mg (4%)**

Greek Almond Cookies (Amygdalota)

Makes 30 cookies

PREP TIME: 30 minutes • **COOK TIME:** 15 minutes • **TOTAL TIME:** 45 minutes
Level 2: Easy

Amygdalota, also known as Greek Almond Macaroons or Biscuits, are simple to make and have only eight Ingredients! Best of all, these cookies are gluten-free, as the recipe calls for almond flour instead of traditional flour.

INGREDIENTS

1 cup slivered almonds

3 cups almond flour

½ cup granulated sugar

¼ cup brown sugar

Zest of 1 lemon

1 teaspoon ground cinnamon

¼ teaspoon salt

3 large egg whites

INSTRUCTIONS

1. Preheat oven to 350°F and line 2 cookie sheets with parchment paper.

2. Place the slivered almonds in a small bowl and set aside.

3. Whisk together the flour, granulated sugar, brown sugar, lemon zest, cinnamon, and salt in a medium bowl.

4. Add the egg whites and stir, until a wet paste-like dough forms.

5. Roll tablespoons of the cookie batter into balls. Roll each ball into the slivered almonds.

6. Place the balls onto the prepared cookie sheet 1-inch apart and flatten each slightly with the palm of your hand.

7. Bake both cookie sheets for 7 minutes, then rotate them and bake an additional 6–8 minutes, until slightly golden.

8. Cool cookies in the pan for 10 minutes, and then transfer to a wire rack to cool completely.

9. Serve once cooled. Refrigerate leftovers in an airtight container for up to 3 days.

NUTRITION · PER ONE SERVING

Calories **98 (4%)**
Total Fat **6.55 g (13%)**
  Saturated Fat **0.498 g**
  Polyunsaturated Fat **1.615 g**
  Monounsaturated Fat **4.133 g**
  Trans Fat **0.002 g**
Cholesterol **0 mg**
Sodium **26 mg (2%)**
Total Carbohydrate: **8.08 g (3%)**
  Dietary Fiber: **1.7 g (7%)**
  Total Sugars: **5.71 g**

Protein: **3.14 g (6%)**
Vitamin A **1 mcg**
Vitamin C **0.3 mcg**
Vitamin D **0 mcg**
Potassium **105 mg (2%)**
Calcium **38 mg (4%)**
Iron **0.5 mg (3%)**

Mandarin Orange Galette

Makes 6 servings

PREP TIME: 30 minutes • **COOK TIME:** 30 minutes • **TOTAL TIME:** 2 hours

Level 4: Challenging

French galettes—free form tarts made with a single crust—are rustic, yet elegant desserts that don't take much effort to make. This galette stars mandarin oranges tossed with cardamom, cinnamon, and ginger. Baked until golden, each bite delivers the perfect balance of warm citrus and fragrant spice enveloped in a flaky crust.

INGREDIENTS

For the crust:

2½ cups all-purpose flour

2 tablespoons granulated sugar

½ teaspoon sea salt

1 cup unsalted butter, cold and diced

6–8 tablespoons ice water

For the galette:

½ cup granulated sugar

Zest of 1 mandarin orange

1 teaspoon ground cinnamon

½ teaspoon ground cardamom

½ teaspoon ground ginger

6 mandarin oranges

1 large egg

1 tablespoon milk

INSTRUCTIONS

To make the crust:

1. Whisk together the flour, sugar, and salt in a medium bowl.

2. Rub the butter into the flour mixture with your fingers until it resembles coarse crumbs.

3. Add the ice water 1 tablespoon at a time, mixing until a dough forms.

4. Transfer the dough onto a lightly floured surface and shape it into a ball. Flatten to form a circle and cover with plastic wrap. Place flattened dough onto a cookie sheet lined with parchment paper. Transfer cookie sheet to the fridge and chill dough for 1 hour.

To make the galette:

1. Preheat oven to 400°F.

2. Combine the sugar, orange zest, cinnamon, cardamom, and ginger in a large bowl, mixing well.

3. Peel and remove the pith and membranes from all oranges. With a sharp knife carefully cut the orange segments in half, lengthwise.

4. Add oranges to the bowl of spices and gently toss to coat.

5. Remove dough from refrigerator with the parchment paper kept underneath. Place down and layer another sheet of parchment paper on top. Roll the dough into a 10-inch circle, ¼-inch thick.

6. Remove the top sheet of parchment paper and transfer the crust on bottom layer of parchment back to the cookie sheet.

7. Arrange the mandarin oranges on the piecrust, leaving a 1½-inch border.

recipe continues

8. Fold the border to meet the edges of the orange slices and press lightly to seal in place.

9. Whisk together the egg and milk in a cup and brush it onto the border of the galette.

10. Bake galette for 30 minutes, until the crust is golden. Cool on a wire rack for 10 minutes before serving.

11. Serve warm or at room temperature. Refrigerate leftovers in an airtight container for up to 3 days.

NUTRITION · PER ONE SERVING

Calories **487 (22%)**	Protein: **8.8 g (16%)**
Total Fat **22.13 g (46%)**	Vitamin A **998 mcg (43%)**
Saturated Fat **13.224 g**	Vitamin C **55 mcg (73%)**
Polyunsaturated Fat **1.178 g**	Vitamin D **22 mcg (4%)**
Monounsaturated Fat **6.35 g**	Potassium **300 mg (6%)**
Trans Fat **0.003 g**	Calcium **84 mg (8%)**
Cholesterol **71 mg**	Iron **3.16 mg (18%)**
Sodium **222 mg (15%)**	
Total Carbohydrate: **64.65 g (26%)**	
Dietary Fiber: **4.3 g (17%)**	
Total Sugars: **21.76 g**	

Fig Walnut Bundt Cake

Makes 10 servings

PREP TIME: 20 minutes • **COOK TIME:** 40 minutes • **TOTAL TIME:** 1 hour
Level 2: Easy

Who knew fresh figs could turn into an appetizing Mediterranean-inspired Bundt cake? With toasted walnuts for added crunch and texture, this cake Makes a fluffy and sweet treat. One slice of this dangerously delicious Fig Walnut Bundt Cake will lift you up to cake heaven.

INGREDIENTS

- 2 cups all-purpose flour
- 2 teaspoons baking powder
- 1 teaspoon salt
- 1 teaspoon ground cinnamon
- ½ teaspoon ginger
- ½ teaspoon cloves
- 1½ cups granulated sugar
- 1 cup butter, melted
- 1 cup buttermilk
- 3 large eggs, lightly beaten
- 1 teaspoon vanilla extract
- 10–12 figs, chopped
- ½ cup walnuts, chopped and toasted

INSTRUCTIONS

1. Preheat oven to 350°F and coat a Bundt pan with non-stick spray.

2. Whisk together the flour, baking powder, salt, cinnamon, ginger, and cloves in a large bowl. Set aside.

3. Whisk together the sugar, butter, buttermilk, eggs, and vanilla extract in a medium bowl.

4. Make a well in the flour mixture and pour in the wet Ingredients. Mix just until incorporated.

5. Fold in the figs and walnuts.

recipe continues

6. Pour batter into the prepared pan and bake for 35–40 minutes, until a skewer comes out clean.

7. Cool the cake in the pan for 5–8 minutes before inverting on a wire rack to finish cooling completely. Serve and enjoy! Refrigerate leftovers in an airtight container for up to 3 days.

NUTRITION · PER ONE SERVING

Calories **471 (22%)**
Total Fat **23.09 g (48%)**
  Saturated Fat **12.588 g**
  Polyunsaturated Fat **3.06 g**
  Monounsaturated Fat **5.801 g**
  Trans Fat **0.759 g**
Cholesterol **106 mg**
Sodium **377 mg (25%)**
Total Carbohydrate: **62.08 g (25%)**
  Dietary Fiber: **2.7 g (11%)**
  Total Sugars: **40.36 g**

Protein: **6.52 g (12%)**
Vitamin A **740 mcg (32%)**
Vitamin C **1.4 mcg (2%)**
Vitamin D **26 mcg (4%)**
Potassium **240 mg (5%)**
Calcium **141 mg (14%)**
Iron **1.93 mg (14%)**

MAIN DESSERTS

Cranberry Mandarin Orange Bread

Makes 10 servings

PREP TIME: 30 minutes • **COOK TIME:** 40 minutes • **TOTAL TIME:** 1 hour 10 minutes
Level 3: Moderate

Cranberries and fresh mandarin oranges come together to form this moist and fluffy loaf. Best of all, it's an effortless dessert that anyone can make. Bake this once and I guarantee it will be at the top of your dessert list. Serve it after dinner or with a cup of tea, and your loved ones will think you spent all day in the kitchen!

INGREDIENTS

2¾ cups all-purpose flour

2 teaspoons baking powder

1 teaspoon ground cardamom

½ teaspoon sea salt

¼ teaspoon baking soda

1¾ cups granulated sugar

¾ cup buttermilk

¾ cup Greek yogurt

½ cup extra-virgin olive oil

2 large eggs

2 cups dried cranberries

2 mandarin oranges, peeled and segmented

INSTRUCTIONS

1. Preheat oven to 350°F and coat a 9-×-5-inch loaf pan with non-stick spray, set aside.

2. Whisk together the flour, baking powder, cardamom, salt, and baking soda in a large bowl.

3. Whisk together the sugar, buttermilk, Greek yogurt, olive oil, and eggs in a separate medium bowl.

4. Make a well in the flour mixture and pour in the wet Ingredients, mixing just until incorporated.

5. Gently fold in the cranberries and mandarin oranges.

6. Pour the mixture into the prepared pan and bake for 35–40 minutes, until a skewer comes out clean.

7. Cool in the pan for 10 minutes, then transfer to a wire rack to cool completely.

8. Serve warm or at room temperature! Refrigerate leftovers in an airtight container for up to 3 days.

NUTRITION · PER ONE SERVING

Calories **360 (16%)**	Protein: **5.56 g (10%)**
Total Fat **13.02 g (27%)**	Vitamin A **143 mcg (6%)**
Saturated Fat **2.583 g**	Vitamin C **34.4 mcg (46%)**
Polyunsaturated Fat **6.644 g**	Vitamin D **8 mcg (1%)**
Monounsaturated Fat **3.146 g**	Potassium **154 mg (3%)**
Trans Fat **0.065 g**	Calcium **136 mg (14%)**
Cholesterol **40 mg**	Iron **1.93 mg (11%)**
Sodium **269 mg (18%)**	
Total Carbohydrate: **56.01 g (23%)**	
Dietary Fiber: **1.7 g (7%)**	
Total Sugars: **27.55 g**	

Maple Fig Shortbread Tart

Makes 6 servings

PREP TIME: 20 minutes • **COOK TIME:** 25 minutes • **TOTAL TIME:** 45 minutes
Level 3: Moderate

This Mediterranean twist on Scottish shortbread ties maple and figs together. The fiber-rich figs are trapped between a flaky layer of vanilla-flavored crust, creating an equally stunning and delicious dessert. This Maple Fig Shortbread Tart is best served with vanilla ice cream if you want to enhance the maple flavor.

INGREDIENTS

- 10–14 fresh figs
- 2⅔ cups all-purpose flour
- ½ cup granulated sugar
- 1 teaspoon baking powder
- ½ teaspoon ground cinnamon
- ½ teaspoon ground cardamom
- ½ teaspoon salt
- 1 cup unsalted butter, cold and cubed
- ⅓ cup unsweetened applesauce
- 2 teaspoons vanilla extract
- ½ cup powdered sugar
- ¼ cup maple syrup
- 2 tablespoons milk

INSTRUCTIONS

1. Preheat oven to 375°F and coat an 8-inch tart pan with a removable bottom with non-stick spray.

2. Destem and cut the figs into ¼-inch slices and set aside.

3. Whisk together the flour, sugar, baking powder, cinnamon, cardamom, and salt in a medium bowl.

4. Add the unsalted butter, applesauce, and vanilla extract to the flour mixture using a pastry cutter or your fingers, until well blended and the texture resembles coarse crumbs.

5. Press ⅔ of the crumb mixture into the bottom and sides of the prepared tart pan to form the crust.

6. Arrange the fig slices in an even layer on the crust.

7. Sprinkle the remaining crumbs evenly over the figs and bake for 20–25 minutes, until golden brown. Allow it to cool.

8. Whisk together the powdered sugar, maple syrup, and milk in a small bowl, forming a smooth, thick glaze.

9. Drizzle the glaze over the thoroughly cooled tart. Serve and enjoy! Refrigerate leftovers in an airtight container for up to 3 days.

NUTRITION · PER ONE SERVING

Calories **544 (25%)**
Total Fat **21.48 g (44%)**
  Saturated Fat **13.022 g**
  Polyunsaturated Fat **1.071 g**
  Monounsaturated Fat **6.066 g**
  Trans Fat **0 g**
Cholesterol **40 mg**
Sodium **278 mg (19%)**
Total Carbohydrate: **81.88 g (33%)**
  Dietary Fiber: **3.6 g (14%)**
  Total Sugars: **34.65 g**

Protein: **7.88 g (14%)**
Vitamin A **648 mcg (28%)**
Vitamin C **0.4 mcg (1%)**
Vitamin D **15 mcg (3%)**
Potassium **254 mg (5%)**
Calcium **133 mg (13%)**
Iron **13.56 mg (20%)**

MAIN DESSERTS

Pistachio Pomegranate Loaf

Makes 10 servings

PREP TIME: 25 minutes • **COOK TIME:** 40 minutes • **TOTAL TIME:** 1 hour 5 minutes
Level 2: Easy

An unlikely combination of pistachios and pomegranate magically combine to form this vegan, gluten-free treasure. Loaded with vitamins and anti-inflammatory properties, you'll also be surprised to know it's as healthy as it is tasty! The appetizingly bright colors of the pomegranates and pistachios will make you fall in love before you even take your first bite.

INGREDIENTS

1 cup unsalted, shelled pistachios, ground

⅔ cup brown rice flour

3 tablespoons millet flour

1 tablespoon tapioca starch

1 teaspoon baking powder

¼ teaspoon sea salt

¼ teaspoon ground cinnamon

¼ teaspoon ground ginger

½ cup pomegranate yogurt

⅓ cup maple syrup

¼ cup pomegranate seeds

2 tablespoons powdered sugar

INSTRUCTIONS

1. Preheat oven to 350°F and coat a 9-×-5-inch loaf pan with non-stick cooking spray.

2. Whisk together the ground pistachios, brown rice flour, millet flour, tapioca starch, baking powder, salt, cinnamon, and ginger in a large bowl.

3. Whisk together the pomegranate yogurt and maple syrup in a separate small bowl and add to the flour mixture, stirring until just combined.

4. Fold in the pomegranate seeds and pour batter into the prepared loaf pan.

5. Bake for 35–40 minutes, until a skewer comes out clean.

6. Cool loaf in pan for 5 minutes, and transfer to a wire rack to cool completely.

7. Dust cooled loaf with powdered sugar and serve immediately. Refrigerate leftovers in an airtight container for up to 3 days.

NUTRITION · PER ONE SERVING

Calories **171 (8%)**	Protein: **4.25 g (8%)**
Total Fat **6.02 g (12%)**	Vitamin A **34 mcg (1%)**
Saturated Fat **0.766 g**	Vitamin C **1.2 mcg (2%)**
Polyunsaturated Fat **1.827 g**	Vitamin D **0 mcg**
Monounsaturated Fat **3.054 g**	Potassium **223 mg (5%)**
Trans Fat **0 g**	Calcium **79 mg (8%)**
Cholesterol **0 mg**	Iron **0.91 mg (5%)**
Sodium **105 mg (7%)**	
Total Carbohydrate: **26.62 g (11%)**	
Dietary Fiber: **2.1 g (8%)**	
Total Sugars: **12.26 g**	

Chocolate Avocado Mousse

Makes 4 servings

PREP TIME: 10 min • **COOK TIME:** 0 • **TOTAL TIME:** 1 hour 10 minutes
Level 1: Very Easy

Yes, you can make a delectable mousse with avocados! This creamy chocolaty treat is so good you won't be able to tell it from the original. What's more, its far healthier, vegan, and gluten-free. Thanks to the avocados, you'll be a whole lot closer to achieving your daily intake of vitamins B and C, and omega-3s.

INGREDIENTS

- 2 large ripe avocados
- ¼ cup cocoa powder
- ¼ cup maple syrup
- 1 tablespoon coconut milk
- 1 teaspoon vanilla extract
- 1 teaspoon instant espresso powder

INSTRUCTIONS

1. Run a knife lengthwise around the perimeter of each avocado, twist it apart, and remove the pit. Scoop the flesh into a food processor's bowl along with the rest of the Ingredients.

2. Process until smooth and creamy, scraping the sides of the bowl as necessary. Divide evenly into 4 dessert dishes and refrigerate for 30–60 minutes, until set.

3. Serve and enjoy! Refrigerate leftovers in an airtight container for up to 3 days.

NUTRITION • PER ONE SERVING

Calories **230 (11%)**
Total Fat **15.58 g (32%)**
  Saturated Fat **2.626 g**
  Polyunsaturated Fat **1.862 g**
  Monounsaturated Fat **10.117 g**
  Trans Fat **0 g**
Cholesterol **0 mg**
Sodium **14 mg (1%)**
Total Carbohydrate: **25.94 g (11%)**
  Dietary Fiber: **8.4 g (34%)**
  Total Sugars: **13.43 g**

Protein: **3.21 g (6%)**
Vitamin A **153 mcg (7%)**
Vitamin C **10.1 mcg (13%)**
Vitamin D **0 mcg**
Potassium **674 mg (14%)**
Calcium **43 mg (4%)**
Iron **1.45 mg (8%)**

Mango Mousse

Makes 4 servings

PREP TIME: 10 minutes • **COOK TIME:** 0 • **TOTAL TIME:** 1 hour 10 minutes
Level 2: Easy

This vegan-friendly mousse is lusciously sweet and creamy, flavored with mint extract and coconut cream, drawing inspiration from the fragrant essences experienced near the Mediterranean Sea. The immune-boosting mango purée is also rich in vitamin C and antioxidants!

INGREDIENTS

1½ cups coconut cream

2 tablespoons powdered sugar

2 tablespoons maple syrup

1½ cups mango purée

1 teaspoon mint extract

½ teaspoon vanilla extract

INSTRUCTIONS

1. Using an electric mixer outfitted with a whisk attachment, blend the coconut cream, powdered sugar, and maple syrup together, until soft peaks form.

2. Fold in the mango purée, mint extract, and vanilla extract.

3. Divide the mousse evenly into 4 serving glasses and refrigerate for 30–60 minutes, until set.

4. Serve and enjoy! Refrigerate leftovers in an airtight container for up to 3 days.

NUTRITION · PER ONE SERVING

Calories **380 (17%)**
Total Fat **31.45 g (65%)**
   Saturated Fat **27.735 g**
   Polyunsaturated Fat **0.387 g**
   Monounsaturated Fat **1.415 g**
   Trans Fat **0 g**
Cholesterol **0 mg**
Sodium **6 mg**
Total Carbohydrate: **26.15 g (11%)**
   Dietary Fiber: **3 g (12%)**
   Total Sugars: **18.61 g**

Protein: **3.78 g (7%)**
Vitamin A **669 mcg (29%)**
Vitamin C **25 mcg (32%)**
Vitamin D **0 mcg**
Potassium **420 mg (9%)**
Calcium **27 mg (3%)**
Iron **2.17 mg (12%)**

Clementine Coconut Panna Cotta

Makes 4 servings

PREP TIME: 20 minutes • **COOK TIME:** 6 minutes • **TOTAL TIME:** 4 hours 26 minutes

Level 2: Easy

This creamy, luxurious dessert bursts with citrus and coconut. Panna Cotta is a traditional Italian treat made with cream and flavored extracts, and this version follows suit with the bright flavor of clementine juice and zest, adding spark to every bite. Since it only takes 20 minutes to make, the real challenge is waiting for it to set!

INGREDIENTS

1 cup heavy cream, divided

2 teaspoons unflavored gelatin

⅓ cup granulated sugar

Zest of 1 clementine

1 cup coconut milk

Juice of 1 clementine

INSTRUCTIONS

1. Lightly coat 4 ramekins with non-stick cooking spray.

2. Place ½ cup of heavy cream in a saucepan and sprinkle the gelatin on top. Let sit for 3 minutes to thicken.

3. Whisk in the remaining heavy cream, sugar, and clementine zest.

4. Cook the mixture over medium-high heat for 5–6 minutes, whisking constantly until the gelatin dissolves and bubbles appear around the edges of the pan.

5. Remove from the heat and stir in the coconut milk and clementine juice.

6. Divide the panna cotta evenly into the prepared ramekins. Cover each one with plastic wrap and refrigerate for 4–5 hours, until set.

7. To serve, run a knife around the inside of the ramekin to loosen the panna cotta and place in a pan of hot (not boiling) water for 20 seconds.

8. Invert onto a serving plate by securely placing the plate on top of the ramekin and flipping it over.

9. Serve and enjoy! Refrigerate leftovers in an airtight container for up to 3 days.

NUTRITION · PER ONE SERVING

Calories **383 (18%)**
Total Fat **34.12 g (70%)**
  Saturated Fat **24.401 g**
  Polyunsaturated Fat **0.959 g**
  Monounsaturated Fat **6.883 g**
  Trans Fat **0 g**
Cholesterol **82 mg**
Sodium **44 mg (3%)**
Total Carbohydrate: **14.09 g (6%)**
  Dietary Fiber: **0.2 g (1%)**
  Total Sugars: **11.54 g**

Protein: **8.53 g (16%)**
Vitamin A **924 mcg (40%)**
Vitamin C **13.7 mcg (18%)**
Vitamin D **16 mcg (3%)**
Potassium **216 mg (5%)**
Calcium **58 mg (6%)**
Iron **2.02 mg (11%)**

MAIN DESSERTS

Clementine Peach Crumble

Makes 8 servings

PREP TIME: 40 minutes • **COOK TIME:** 45 minutes • **TOTAL TIME:** 1 hour 25 minutes
Level 3: Moderate

The taste of fresh peaches is hard to resist, and this zesty dessert adds an element of spice paired with a buttery, flaky crust, bringing out their best flavors. There is truly nothing better than the aroma of this Clementine Peach Crumble, except eating it! Once you have your first bite, I know you'll agree.

INGREDIENTS

For the filling:

3-4 medium peaches, rinsed and sliced

3 clementines, peeled and segmented

½ cup granulated sugar

1 teaspoon cinnamon

¼ teaspoon nutmeg

¼ teaspoon ground ginger

For the topping:

1 cup all-purpose flour

½ cup granulated sugar

1 teaspoon baking powder

½ teaspoon ground cinnamon

¼ teaspoon salt

⅛ teaspoon nutmeg

½ cup unsalted butter, melted

1 teaspoon vanilla extract

INSTRUCTIONS

To make the filling:

1. Preheat oven to 350ºF and lightly coat a 9-×-12-inch baking dish with non-stick cooking spray.

2. Place the fruit into a medium bowl and add the sugar, cinnamon, nutmeg, and ginger, stirring to combine, then distribute fruit evenly in the prepared baking dish and set aside.

To make the topping:

1. Whisk together the flour, sugar, baking powder, cinnamon, salt, and nutmeg in a small bowl.

2. Add the melted butter and vanilla, tossing lightly with a fork until the mixture resembles coarse crumbs.

3. Sprinkle the crumb mixture evenly over the fruit and bake for 35–45 minutes, or until the fruit is bubbly and the crust is golden.

4. Cool for 10–15 minutes.

5. Serve warm with ice cream or whipped cream, if desired. Refrigerate leftovers in an airtight container for up to 3 days.

NUTRITION · PER ONE SERVING

Calories **247 (11%)**
Total Fat **7.97 g (16%)**
   Saturated Fat **4.861 g**
   Polyunsaturated Fat **0.356 g**
   Monounsaturated Fat **2.252 g**
   Trans Fat **0 g**
Cholesterol **15 mg**
Sodium **124 mg (8%)**
Total Carbohydrate: **42.55 g (17%)**
   Dietary Fiber: **1.3 g (5%)**
   Total Sugars: **29.13 g**

Protein: **2.38 g (4%)**
Vitamin A **259 mcg (11%)**
Vitamin C **20 mcg (27%)**
Vitamin D **6 mcg (1%)**
Potassium **89 mg (2%)**
Calcium **65 mg (7%)**
Iron **1.06 mg (6%)**

Peach Apricot Sherbet

Makes 6 servings

PREP TIME: 10 minutes • **COOK TIME:** 0 • **TOTAL TIME:** 5 hours 10 minutes

Level 2: Easy

Sherbet is ice cream's lighter cousin. Using only 4 simple Ingredients, this fruit-rich frozen treat takes on a beautiful pastel yellow color. With its tangy balance of sweet and tart, this recipe will rival your go-to ice cream.

INGREDIENTS

- 3 large peaches, peeled, pitted, and sliced
- 3 apricots, peeled, pitted, and sliced
- 1 (14-oz.) can sweetened condensed milk
- 1 teaspoon vanilla extract

INSTRUCTIONS

1. Arrange the fruit slices in a single layer on a parchment-lined cookie sheet and freeze for 4–5 hours.

2. In a blender, combine the fruit, condensed milk, and vanilla. Process until smooth and creamy with the texture of soft serve.

3. Serve immediately. Freeze leftovers in an airtight container for up to 3 days.

NUTRITION · PER ONE SERVING

Calories **257 (12%)**
Total Fat **6.05 g (12%)**
  Saturated Fat **3.651 g**
  Polyunsaturated Fat **0.314 g**
  Monounsaturated Fat **1.964 g**
  Trans Fat **0 g**
Cholesterol **22 mg**
Sodium **86 mg (6%)**
Total Carbohydrate: **46.84 g (19%)**
  Dietary Fiber: **1.7 g (7%)**
  Total Sugars: **45.32 g**

Protein: **6.34 g (12%)**
Vitamin A **799 mcg (34%)**
Vitamin C **9.3 mcg (12%)**
Vitamin D **4 mcg (1%)**
Potassium **460 mg (10%)**
Calcium **196 mg (20%)**
Iron **0.44 mg (2%)**

No-Bake Mediterranean Lemon Pie

Makes 8 servings

PREP TIME: 30 minutes • **COOK TIME:** 4 minutes • **TOTAL TIME:** 8 hours 34 minutes

Level 3: Moderate

Lemon brightens any dish, and this No-Bake Mediterranean Lemon Pie is no exception. A crust made from sweetened, crunchy cookies, with a hint of vanilla flavor, and paired with freshly squeezed lemon juice, this may be the best pie you will ever taste.

INGREDIENTS

For the crust:

30 Maria cookies

6 tablespoons butter, melted

1 teaspoon vanilla extract

For the pie filling:

1½ cups water

5 sheets neutral-flavored gelatin

½ cup milk

1 cup heavy cream

14 ounces sweetened condensed milk

½ cup cream cheese

Juice of 3 lemons

Zest of 1 lemon

INSTRUCTIONS

To make the crust:

1. Seal the Maria cookies in a zip-top bag and crush with a mallet or a rolling pin into fine crumbs.

2. In a small bowl, combine the cookie crumbs with the melted butter and vanilla extract. Mix well until mixture sticks together.

3. Press the cookie mixture firmly into the bottom of a 9-inch springform pan and refrigerate for 30 minutes.

To make the filling:

1. Add the water to a bowl and submerge the gelatin sheets. Let them sit for 5 minutes, until they rehydrate.

2. Cook the milk in a saucepan set over medium-high heat for 3–4 minutes, until bubbles appear around the pan's edges. Remove from heat.

recipe continues

3. Remove the gelatin sheets from the water and add to the hot milk, stirring until the gelatin dissolves completely. Cool gelatin until it is warm, but not set, around 15–20 minutes.

4. Combine warm gelatin mixture with the remaining Ingredients in a blender and process until smooth, thick, and creamy.

5. Remove the Maria cookie crust from the fridge and pour in the pie filling.

6. Refrigerate for 6–8 hours, or until set.

7. Serve cold. Refrigerate leftovers in an airtight container for up to 3 days.

NUTRITION · PER ONE SERVING

Calories **483 (22%)**	Protein: **10.2 g (19%)**
Total Fat **34.62 g (71%)**	Vitamin A **869 mcg (37%)**
Saturated Fat **17.817 g**	Vitamin C **8.1 mcg (11%)**
Polyunsaturated Fat **4.586 g**	Vitamin D **17 mcg (3%)**
Monounsaturated Fat **9.494 g**	Potassium **191 mg (4%)**
Trans Fat **0.316 g**	Calcium **122 mg (12%)**
Cholesterol **71 mg**	Iron **1.69 mg (9%)**
Sodium **271 mg (18%)**	
Total Carbohydrate: **34.01 g (14%)**	
Dietary Fiber: **0.7 g (3%)**	
Total Sugars: **17.61 g**	

Apricot Macaroons

Makes 18–20 macaroons

PREP TIME: 45 minutes • **COOK TIME:** 20 minutes • **TOTAL TIME:** 1 hour 5 minutes
Level 2: Easy

Eating these macaroons will seem like an extravagance because they're kissed with Notes of both velvety apricot and savory coconut. The irresistible texture of these slightly crisp macaroons with a moist, chewy interior is sure to wow your guests!

INGREDIENTS

- 4 large egg whites
- ½ cup granulated sugar
- 1 teaspoon vanilla extract
- 4¾ cups sweetened coconut, shredded
- ½ cup apricot, peeled and diced

INSTRUCTIONS

1. Preheat oven to 325°F and line two cookie sheets with parchment paper.

2. Whisk together the egg whites, sugar, and vanilla extract in a large bowl for 2 minutes, until the sugar is dissolved, and the egg whites are foamy.

3. Fold in the shredded coconut until completely coated with the egg white mixture.

4. Cover the bowl with plastic wrap and chill in the fridge for 30 minutes so the coconut absorbs some of the egg mixture.

5. Pat any liquid that has formed from the chopped apricots with paper towels. Remove batter from fridge and fold in the apricots.

6. Scoop 2 tablespoons of batter and place onto the prepared cookie sheet leaving 2-inch spaces between each macaroon.

recipe continues

7. Bake for 15–20 minutes, rotating the cookie sheets at the 10-minute mark, until they are golden brown.

8. Allow the macaroons to cool completely and serve. Refrigerate leftovers in an airtight container for up to 3 days.

NUTRITION · PER ONE SERVING

Calories **134 (6%)**	Protein: **1.37 g (3%)**
Total Fat **7.85 g (16%)**	Vitamin A **17 mcg (1%)**
Saturated Fat **6.952 g**	Vitamin C **0.2 mcg**
Polyunsaturated Fat **0.086 g**	Vitamin D **0 mcg**
Monounsaturated Fat **0.335 g**	Potassium **88 mg (2%)**
Trans Fat **0 g**	Calcium **4 mg**
Cholesterol **0 mg**	Iron **0.44 mg (2%)**
Sodium **69 mg (5%)**	
Total Carbohydrate: **15.7 g (6%)**	
Dietary Fiber: **1 g (4%)**	
Total Sugars: **14.68 g**	

Mediterranean Crêpes

Makes 4 servings

PREP TIME: 10 minutes • **COOK TIME:** 20 minutes • **TOTAL TIME:** 1 hour

Level 3: Moderate

We all know that crêpes are associated with French cuisine. However, these Mediterranean Crêpes are a fresh spin on the classic dish. Serve with fig or apricot preserves, freshly whipped cream, jam, or fresh fruits to maximize flavor—and health benefits!

INGREDIENTS

- 4 cups milk
- 2½ cups all-purpose flour
- 4 large eggs
- 1 teaspoon sunflower oil
- ¼ teaspoon salt
- 1 teaspoon unsalted butter

INSTRUCTIONS

1. Combine all Ingredients, except butter, in a blender and process until smooth.

2. Let the crêpe batter rest for 30 minutes at room temperature.

3. Set a small (7½-inch) frying pan over medium-high heat. Once hot, add the butter, swirling it around the pan to melt.

4. Use a small ladle to scoop enough of the crêpe batter to coat the entire bottom of the pan. Swirl the pan to spread the batter or use the bottom of the ladle.

5. Cook until the crêpe batter dries completely, and the edges pull away from the pan.

6. With a spatula, flip the crêpe over and cook an additional 1–2 minutes, or until golden brown. Transfer each cooked crêpe to a parchment-lined cookie sheet, spread apart so they don't stick together.

7. Fill crêpes with your favorite fillings; whipped cream, preserved fruits, or nut butter. Serve and enjoy!

NOTE: The first crêpe will likely absorb most of the butter, which Makes it oilier than the rest. The remaining crêpes will cook perfectly.

NUTRITION · PER ONE SERVING

Calories **484 (23%)**
Total Fat **12.12 g (25%)**
  Saturated Fat **5.265 g**
  Polyunsaturated Fat **1.523 g**
  Monounsaturated Fat **4.392 g**
  Trans Fat **0.226 g**
Cholesterol **207 mg**
Sodium **333 mg (22%)**
Total Carbohydrate: **71.69 g (29%)**
  Dietary Fiber: **2.1 g (8%)**
  Total Sugars: **12.74 g**

Protein: **22.44 g (41%)**
Vitamin A **754 mcg (32%)**
Vitamin C **0.5 mcg (1%)**
Vitamin D **161 mcg (27%)**
Potassium **465 mg (11%)**
Calcium **333 mg (33%)**
Iron **4.46 mg (25%)**

MAIN DESSERTS

Spiced Orange Ricotta Cake

Makes 12 servings

PREP TIME: 25 minutes • **COOK TIME:** 45 minutes • **TOTAL TIME:** 1 hour 10 minutes
Level 2: Easy

Orange combines with cinnamon, allspice, and clove, loading this delightfully fragrant, fluffy, and moist cake with flavor. This recipe works with any variety of orange you have on hand—from Navel to Seville, and even blood oranges! Whichever you choose, this cake will brighten your day.

INGREDIENTS

- ½ cup brown sugar
- 4 tablespoons unsalted butter, melted and divided
- 1 orange, thinly sliced
- 1½ cups all-purpose flour
- 2 teaspoons baking powder
- 1 teaspoon ground cinnamon
- ½ teaspoon sea salt
- ¼ teaspoon ground cloves
- ⅛ teaspoon allspice
- 1½ cups ricotta cheese
- ¾ cup granulated sugar
- 3 large eggs
- ¼ cup extra-virgin olive oil
- Zest of 1 orange
- 1 teaspoon vanilla extract
- ½ teaspoon almond extract

INSTRUCTIONS

1. Preheat oven to 325°F and line a 9-inch cake pan with parchment paper.

2. Combine the brown sugar and 2 tablespoons of the melted butter in a small bowl, mixing well, until a thick paste forms.

3. Spread the mixture onto the prepared pan's bottom, lined with parchment paper. Once the bottom is coated with the paste, arrange the orange slices on top.

4. Whisk together the flour, baking powder, cinnamon, salt, cloves, and allspice in a bowl.

5. In a separate bowl, whisk together the remaining Ingredients and the remaining 2 tablespoons of butter.

6. Combine the dry and wet Ingredients, mixing until completely incorporated.

7. Pour batter into the prepared cake pan and bake for 40–45 minutes, until a skewer comes out clean.

8. Cool in the pan for 5 minutes and then run a knife around the perimeter of the pan to loosen cake before inverting it onto a serving dish.

9. Peel off the parchment paper and let the cake cool completely before serving. Refrigerate leftovers in an airtight container for up to 3 days.

NUTRITION · PER ONE SERVING

Calories **237 (11%)**
Total Fat **12.43 g (26%)**
   Saturated Fat **5.232 g**
   Polyunsaturated Fat **0.944 g**
   Monounsaturated Fat **5.684 g**
   Trans Fat **0.002 g**
Cholesterol **67 mg**
Sodium **188 mg (13%)**
Total Carbohydrate: **25.46 g (10%)**
   Dietary Fiber: **0.9 g (4%)**
Total Sugars: **11.38 g**

Protein: **6.07 g (11%)**
Vitamin A **310 mcg (13%)**
Vitamin C **7.5 mcg (10%)**
Vitamin D **14 mcg (2%)**
Potassium **81 mg (2%)**
Calcium **139 mg (14%)**
Iron **1.18 mg (7%)**

MAIN DESSERTS

Brûléed Berry Mascarpone

Makes 4 servings

PREP TIME: 20 minutes • **COOK TIME:** 10 minutes • **TOTAL TIME:** 30 minutes
Level 3: Moderate

Creamy mascarpone cheese is sweetened with maple syrup and infused with vanilla and orange in this Mediterranean-inspired version of Crème Brûlée. This elegant dessert boasts the creaminess and crunchy topping of its traditional French namesake—but without all the hard work.

INGREDIENTS

- 1½ cups mascarpone cheese
- 2 tablespoons maple syrup
- 1 tablespoon vanilla extract
- Zest of 1 orange
- 2 tablespoons granulated sugar
- 16 blackberries

INSTRUCTIONS

1. Set oven to broil on high.

2. Combine the mascarpone cheese, maple syrup, vanilla extract, and orange zest in a bowl, mixing well.

3. Divide the mixture evenly into 4 (6-oz.) ramekins arranged on a rimmed cookie sheet.

4. Sprinkle the top of each ramekin with ½ tablespoon of granulated sugar and broil until the tops are a golden brown, about 5–10 minutes.

5. Remove from the oven and cool for 10 minutes before topping with blackberries. Refrigerate leftovers in an airtight container for up to 3 days.

NUTRITION • PER ONE SERVING

Calories **376 (17%)**	Protein: **5.37 g (10%)**
Total Fat **29.89 g (62%)**	Vitamin A **1182 mcg (51%)**
Saturated Fat **16.792 g**	Vitamin C **9.3 mcg (12%)**
Polyunsaturated Fat **1.294 g**	Vitamin D **22 mcg (4%)**
Monounsaturated Fat **7.514 g**	Potassium **174 mg (4%)**
Trans Fat **0 g**	Calcium **101 mg (10%)**
Cholesterol **96 mg**	Iron **0.46 mg (3%)**
Sodium **320 mg (21%)**	
Total Carbohydrate: **21.73 g (9%)**	
Dietary Fiber: **0.7 g (3%)**	
Total Sugars: **19.35 g**	

MAIN DESSERTS

Baked Plums with Pecans & Maple Syrup

Makes 4 servings

PREP TIME: 25 minutes • **COOK TIME:** 30 minutes • **TOTAL TIME:** 55 minutes
Level 2: Easy

Six simple Ingredients, five of which are probably already in your pantry, create a dessert that no one will believe was this simple to make. The spices bring out the best in the plums and the nuts boost your calcium, potassium, and magnesium intake, while adding a satisfying crunchy texture.

INGREDIENTS

4 plums, pitted and cut in half

14 teaspoons ground cardamom

1 teaspoon ground cinnamon

½ teaspoon nutmeg

¼ cup pecans, crushed

4 teaspoons maple syrup

INSTRUCTIONS

1. Preheat oven to 350°F.

2. Arrange the plums cut side up on a rimmed cookie sheet.

3. Whisk together the cardamom, cinnamon, and nutmeg in a cup or small bowl.

4. Sprinkle the spices over the plums, then place ½ tablespoon of crushed pecans in the center of each plum.

5. Drizzle each plum with ½ teaspoon of maple syrup and bake for 30 minutes.

6. Remove from the oven and cool baked plums for 10–15 minutes.

7. Serve warm. Top with ice cream or whipped cream, if desired. Refrigerate leftovers in an airtight container for up to 3 days.

NUTRITION · PER ONE SERVING

Calories **115 (5%)**
Total Fat **5.23 g (11%)**
   Saturated Fat **0.516 g**
   Polyunsaturated Fat **1.402 g**
   Monounsaturated Fat **2.69 g**
   Trans Fat **0 g**
Cholesterol **0 mg**
Sodium **2 mg**
Total Carbohydrate: **18.24 g (7%)**
   Dietary Fiber: **3.9 g (16%)**
   Total Sugars: **10.78 g**

Protein: **1.83 g (3%)**
Vitamin A **233 mcg (10%)**
Vitamin C **7.8 mcg (10%)**
Vitamin D **0 mcg**
Potassium **225 mg (5%)**
Calcium **49 mg (5%)**
Iron **1.32 mg (7%)**

Olive Oil Pecan Banana Bread

Makes 12 servings

PREP TIME: 40 minutes • **COOK TIME:** 1 hour • **TOTAL TIME:** 1 hour 40 minutes
Level 2: Easy

Banana bread is a quick and classic dessert that never fails to satisfy everyone at the table. In this egg-free version, Greek yogurt and pecans add protein and fiber, which keeps you feeling full! The best part? It's lower in calories than traditional banana bread recipes, but just as delicious.

INGREDIENTS

- 1 cup all-purpose flour
- ½ cup almond flour
- 1 teaspoon baking soda
- ¾ teaspoon salt
- 3 medium bananas, mashed
- ½ cup granulated sugar
- ¼ cup extra-virgin olive oil
- ¼ cup plain Greek yogurt
- ¼ cup brown sugar, packed
- 1 teaspoon vanilla extract
- 1 teaspoon almond extract
- ¼ cup pecans, chopped

INSTRUCTIONS

1. Preheat oven to 325°F and coat a 9-×-5-inch loaf pan with non-stick cooking spray.

2. Whisk together both flours, baking soda, and salt in a medium bowl.

3. Whisk together the remaining Ingredients, except the pecans, in a separate large bowl.

4. Add the dry Ingredients to the mashed banana mixture, stirring just until incorporated.

5. Fold in the pecans and pour the batter into the prepared pan.

6. Bake for 45–60 minutes, until a skewer comes out clean.

recipe continues

7. Cool in the pan for 15 minutes, then place on a wire rack to cool completely. Serve warm or at room temperature! Refrigerate leftovers in an airtight container for up to 3 days.

NUTRITION · PER ONE SERVING

Calories **116 (8%)**
Total Fat **7.83 g (16%)**
  Saturated Fat **0.933 g**
  Polyunsaturated Fat **1.825 g**
  Monounsaturated Fat **4.734 g**
  Trans Fat **0.003 g**
Cholesterol **0 mg**
Sodium **301 mg (20%)**
Total Carbohydrate: **22.24 g (9%)**
  Dietary Fiber: **1.7 g (7%)**
  Total Sugars: **10.17 g**

Protein: **2.99 g (5%)**
Vitamin A **19 mcg (1%)**
Vitamin C **2.6 mcg (3%)**
Vitamin D **0 mcg**
Potassium **161 mg (3%)**
Calcium **21 mg (2%)**
Iron **0.79 mg (4%)**

Greek Milk Pie (Galatopita)

Makes 6 servings

PREP TIME: 50 minutes • **COOK TIME:** 1 hour 5 minutes • **TOTAL TIME:** 1 hour 55 minutes
Level 4: Challenging

This pie is a classic Greek dessert that's very easy to make. It has a delicate, crispy and buttery phyllo dough crust paired with a divinely creamy, sweet filling that will make you fall in love. Note that people who cannot tolerate cow's milk usually experience no digestive issues with goat's milk!

INGREDIENTS

For the filling:

4 cups whole goat's milk

½ cup unsalted goat butter

½ cup granulated sugar

½ cup honey

1 tablespoon vanilla extract

Zest of 1 lemon

1 teaspoon ground cinnamon

¼ teaspoon sea salt

½ cup finely ground semolina

5 eggs, lightly beaten

For the phyllo dough:

2 tablespoons ground cinnamon

2 tablespoons granulated sugar

1 teaspoon nutmeg

5 sheets phyllo pastry, thawed

¼ cup unsalted goat butter, melted

INSTRUCTIONS

To make the filling:

1. Preheat oven to 350°F and coat a 12-inch tart pan with non-stick spray. Unroll the phyllo dough onto a dry, level surface such as a pastry board.

2. Combine the goat's milk and butter in a saucepan set over medium-high heat for 4–5 minutes, until bubbles form around the edge of the pan.

3. Add the sugar, honey, vanilla extract, lemon zest, cinnamon, and salt, stirring to combine.

4. Decrease heat to medium-low and slowly add the semolina while stirring constantly. Continue cooking for 10–15 minutes, stirring constantly. Once the custard thickens, remove from heat and cool for 5 minutes.

5. Add a few tablespoons of the hot custard to the beaten eggs, preventing them from curdling, then add the eggs to the custard, constantly whisking.

recipe and ingredients continue

For the topping:

1 egg, slightly beaten

2 tablespoons water

2 tablespoons granulated sugar

To make the phyllo dough:

1. While the custard cools, whisk together the cinnamon, sugar, and nutmeg in a small bowl.

2. Place a sheet of the phyllo into the prepared tart pan, brush the entire sheet with melted butter, and sprinkle with some of the sugar mixture. Top with another sheet of phyllo and repeat until you run out of phyllo.

3. Pour the custard into the tart pan and smooth into an even layer. Trim any excess phyllo hanging over the edge with a knife or kitchen shears.

4. Fold or pinch dough to create a decorative edge. Set aside.

To make the topping:

1. Whisk together the egg, water, and sugar in a small bowl, until well blended, then pour it over the custard.

2. Bake for 45 minutes, until the phyllo is golden.

3. Cool on a rack for 30 minutes. Serve and enjoy! Refrigerate leftovers in an airtight container for up to 3 days.

NUTRITION · PER ONE SERVING

Calories **574 (26%)**

Total Fat **27.92 g (29%)**
  Saturated Fat **14.738 g**
  Polyunsaturated Fat **2.04 g**
  Monounsaturated Fat **8.602 g**
  Trans Fat **0.282 g**

Cholesterol **304 mg**

Sodium **332 mg (22%)**

Total Carbohydrate: **67.11 g (27%)**
  Dietary Fiber: **2.6 g (10%)**
  Total Sugars: **45.62 g**

Protein: **15.92 g (29%)**

Vitamin A **1052 mcg (45%)**

Vitamin C **3.4 mcg (5%)**

Vitamin D **136 mcg (23%)**

Potassium **396 mg (8%)**

Calcium **266 mg (27%)**

Iron **2.61 mg (15%)**

Carrot Cake

Makes 10 servings

PREP TIME: 40 minutes • **COOK TIME:** 40 minutes • **TOTAL TIME:** 1 hour 20 minutes
Level 2: Easy

Made with fresh carrots and studded with dried apricots and prunes, this unusual combination of Ingredients evolves into the moistest and most flavorful Carrot Cake you'll ever eat. The earthy spices intensify the flavor, elevating this recipe to a whole new level.

INGREDIENTS

- 2 cups carrots, shredded
- 1 cup oat flour
- 1 cup whole wheat flour
- 1 tablespoon ground cinnamon
- 2 teaspoons baking soda
- ½ teaspoon nutmeg
- ¼ teaspoon ground cloves
- 1 cup unsweetened applesauce
- 4 large eggs
- ½ cup granulated sugar
- ½ cup honey
- ½ cup sour cream
- 1 teaspoon vanilla extract
- ¼ cup dried apricots
- ¼ cup prunes

INSTRUCTIONS

1. Preheat oven to 350°F and coat a 9-×-5-inch loaf pan with non-stick spray.

2. Place shredded carrots on a paper towel-lined plate to absorb excess moisture and set aside.

3. Whisk together both flours, cinnamon, baking soda, nutmeg, and cloves together in a medium bowl.

4. Combine the unsweetened applesauce, eggs, sugar, honey, sour cream, and vanilla extract in a separate large bowl, mixing well.

5. Add the dry Ingredients to applesauce mixture, stirring just until incorporated.

6. Fold in the shredded carrots, dried apricots, and prunes.

7. Pour the batter into the prepared loaf pan. Bake for 35–40 minutes, until a skewer comes out clean.

8. Cool in the pan for 5–10 minutes, then transfer to a wire rack to cool completely. Serve and enjoy! Refrigerate leftovers in an airtight container for up to 3 days.

NUTRITION · PER ONE SERVING

Calories **192 (9%)**
Total Fat **3.72 g (8%)**
  Saturated Fat **1.399 g**
  Polyunsaturated Fat **0.737 g**
  Monounsaturated Fat **1.267 g**
  Trans Fat **0.001 g**
Cholesterol **65 mg**
Sodium **389 mg (26%)**
Total Carbohydrate: **37.57 g (15%)**
  Dietary Fiber: **3.1 g (12%)**
  Total Sugars: **19.07 g**

Protein: **4.6 g (8%)**
Vitamin A **3429 mcg (147%)**
Vitamin C **1.2 mcg (2%)**
Vitamin D **13 mcg (2%)**
Potassium **287 mg (6%)**
Calcium **53 mg (5%)**
Iron **1.3 mg (7%)**

Grapefruit Lavender Olive Oil Cake

Makes 8 servings

PREP TIME: 45 minutes • **COOK TIME:** 45 minutes • **TOTAL TIME:** 2 hours
Level 3: Moderate

Olive oil cakes are known for their irresistibly tender crumble and vivid flavor. This cake lives up to that pedigree, infused with freshly squeezed grapefruit juice and zest and fragrant lavender extract. As an added bonus, grapefruit is also known for its ability to protect cells from harmful bacteria.

INGREDIENTS

- 1¼ cups cake flour
- ½ cup fine cornmeal
- 2 tablespoons grapefruit zest
- 2 teaspoons baking powder
- ¼ teaspoon baking soda
- ¼ teaspoon salt
- ⅔ cup granulated sugar
- ¼ cup grapefruit juice
- 3 large eggs
- ½ cup plain Greek yogurt
- ½ cup extra-virgin olive oil
- 1 teaspoon lavender extract

INSTRUCTIONS

1. Move the rack to the center of the oven.

2. Preheat oven to 350°F and coat a 9-×-5-inch loaf pan with non-stick cooking spray.

3. Whisk together the flour, cornmeal, grapefruit zest, baking powder, baking soda, and salt in a medium bowl and set it aside.

4. Whisk together the sugar and grapefruit juice in a large bowl. Once combined, add the eggs, yogurt, olive oil, and lavender extract, mixing well.

5. Add the dry Ingredients to the grapefruit juice mixture and stir just until combined.

6. Pour the batter into the prepared loaf pan. Bake for 40–45 minutes, until a skewer comes out clean.

7. Remove from oven and allow cake to cool for 5 minutes. Gently remove the cake from the pan and transfer to a wire rack to cool completely, about 25–30 minutes.

8. As an option you can decorate the cake with your favorite glaze, icing or cream. Serve and enjoy!

NUTRITION · PER ONE SERVING

Calories **415 (19%)**
Total Fat **16.1 g (33%)**
  Saturated Fat **2.656 g**
  Polyunsaturated Fat **2.009 g**
  Monounsaturated Fat **10.738 g**
  Trans Fat **0.007 g**
Cholesterol **70 mg**
Sodium **305 mg (20%)**
Total Carbohydrate: **61.62 g (25%)**
  Dietary Fiber: **1.5 g (6%)**
  Total Sugars: **37.8 g**

Protein: **6.26 g (11%)**
Vitamin A **518 mcg (22%)**
Vitamin C **9.6 mcg (13%)**
Vitamin D **14 mcg (2%)**
Potassium **268 mg (6%)**
Calcium **108 mg (11%)**
Iron **1.6 mg (9%)**

Almond Olive Oil Shortbread Crackers

Makes 18–24 crackers

PREP TIME: 15 minutes • **COOK TIME:** 20 minutes • **TOTAL TIME:** 35 minutes
Level 3: Moderate

These Almond Olive Oil Shortbread Crackers may not be the prettiest treat you've ever laid your eyes on, but their taste more than Makes up for it. Bursting with a warm, nutty flavor, serve these crispy crackers with coffee or tea and you've got a relaxing evening to look forward to.

INGREDIENTS

1¼ cups almond flour

¾ cup all-purpose flour

¼ cup brown sugar

¼ cup superfine sugar

Zest of 1 orange

1 teaspoon kosher salt

1 teaspoon ground cinnamon

½ cup extra-virgin olive oil

1 teaspoon vanilla extract

INSTRUCTIONS

1. Preheat oven to 375°F and line the bottom of an 8-×-8-inch baking dish with parchment paper.

2. Whisk together the flours, sugars, orange zest, salt, and cinnamon.

3. Add the olive oil and vanilla extract, mixing well, until a crumbly dough forms.

4. Press dough into the prepared baking dish.

5. Bake for 20 minutes, until the dough starts to brown around the edges.

6. Remove from oven and immediately cut into 18–24 diamond-shaped crackers.

7. Cool crackers completely in the pan before serving. Refrigerate leftover crackers in an airtight container for up to 5 days.

NUTRITION · PER ONE SERVING

Calories **93 (4%)**

Total Fat **7.01 g (14%)**
  Saturated Fat **0.816 g**
  Polyunsaturated Fat **1.101 g**
  Monounsaturated Fat **4.4849 g**
  Trans Fat **0.003 g**

Cholesterol **0 mg**

Sodium **98 mg (7%)**

Total Carbohydrate: **6.42 g (3%)**
  Dietary Fiber: **0.8 g (3%)**

Total Sugars: **2.36 g**

Protein: **1.68 g (3%)**

Vitamin A **1 mcg**

Vitamin C **0.3 mcg**

Vitamin D **0 mcg**

Potassium **42 mg (1%)**

Calcium **16 mg (2%)**

Iron **0.41 mg (2%)**

Cranberry Almond Biscotti

Makes 16 biscotti

PREP TIME: 30 minutes • **COOK TIME:** 41 minutes • **TOTAL TIME:** 1 hour 41 minutes
Level 4: Challenging

Biscotti was invented in the Tuscan region of Prato, Italy. Commonly called Cantucci, these twice-baked flavorful cookies are studded with cranberries, almonds, and lemon zest, while retaining the traditional and satisfying biscotti crunch.

INGREDIENTS

- ¾ cup granulated sugar
- ¼ cup cold unsalted butter
- 2 large eggs
- Zest of 1 lemon
- 1 teaspoon vanilla extract
- 2 cups all-purpose flour
- 1 teaspoon baking powder
- ½ teaspoon sea salt
- ½ cup dried cranberries
- ½ cup almonds, chopped

INSTRUCTIONS

1. Preheat oven to 350°F and line a cookie sheet with parchment paper.

2. Place the sugar and unsalted butter into the bowl of a stand mixer outfitted with the paddle attachment and beat together, until light and fluffy.

3. Add the eggs, lemon zest, and vanilla extract, mixing just until incorporated.

4. Whisk together the flour, baking powder, and salt in a medium bowl and add to the butter mixture, mixing on low speed, until combined.

5. Add the cranberries and almonds and mix on low, just until incorporated.

6. Remove dough to a lightly floured surface and divide in half.

7. Form each half into a ball and the roll each into an 8-inch log.

8. Place biscotti logs side-by-side on prepared cookie sheet and flatten them slightly.

9. Bake for 20–25 minutes, until slightly golden.

10. Allow the biscotti to cool completely for 30 minutes and then cut each log diagonally into 8 slices.

11. Return the cookies to the parchment-lined cookie sheet and arrange cut side up, ½-inch apart to bake for an additional 12–16 minutes, until they dry out.

12. Transfer biscotti to a wire rack to cool completely before serving. Biscotti freeze well and keep their just-baked crunch if stored at room temperature in an airtight container.

NUTRITION · PER ONE SERVING

Calories **133 (6%)**
Total Fat **2.36 g (5%)**
   Saturated Fat **0.408 g**
   Polyunsaturated Fat **0.569 g**
   Monounsaturated Fat **1.192 g**
   Trans Fat **0.003 g**
Cholesterol **23 mg**
Sodium **83 mg (6%)**
Total Carbohydrate: **25.32 g (10%)**
   Dietary Fiber: **1 g (4%)**
   Total Sugars: **12.06 g**

Protein: **3.02 g (6%)**
Vitamin A **38 mcg (2%)**
Vitamin C **0.5 mcg (1%)**
Vitamin D **5 mcg (1%)**
Potassium **81 mg (2%)**
Calcium **28 mg (3%)**
Iron **1 mg (6%)**

Moustokouloura Cookies

Makes 20 cookies

PREP TIME: 35 minutes • **COOK TIME:** 17 minutes • **TOTAL TIME:** 52 minutes
Level 3: Moderate

The Greek word moustokouloura translates to 'grape must cookies,' because grape molasses is used to sweeten these traditional, vegan-friendly cookies. This fragrant treat, bursting with the rich, spicy tones of cinnamon and nutmeg are definitely a must for any table! Traditionally, these cookies are served during Lent, but you're going to want to eat them year-round.

INGREDIENTS

- ¾ cup granulated sugar
- ½ cup + 2 tablespoons grape molasses (Petmezi)
- ½ cup + 2 tablespoons water
- ¾ cup vegetable oil
- ¼ cup extra-virgin olive oil
- 2 tablespoons maple syrup
- 1 teaspoon vanilla extract
- 5 cups cake flour
- 1 teaspoon ground cinnamon
- ½ teaspoon nutmeg
- ½ teaspoon baking soda
- ½ teaspoon baking powder

INSTRUCTIONS

1. Preheat oven to 360°F and line a cookie sheet with parchment paper.

2. Whisk together the sugar, grape molasses, and water in a large bowl.

3. Add the vegetable oil, olive oil, maple syrup, and vanilla extract, whisking for 5 minutes, until well combined.

4. Whisk together the flour, cinnamon, nutmeg, baking soda, and baking powder in another medium bowl.

5. Add the dry Ingredients to the grape molasses mixture and stir until a rough dough forms.

6. Turn dough onto a lightly floured surface and divide into 20 even-sized balls.

7. Roll each ball into a 3-inch rope and bring the edges together to form a circle-shaped cookie.

8. Arrange the cookie circles on the prepared cookie sheet leaving 1-inch of space around each cookie.

9. Bake for 15–17 minutes. Be careful not to overbake—the cookies should be soft and will harden as they cool.

10. Cool cookies on the pan for 5 minutes, then transfer to a wire rack to cool completely. Serve and enjoy! Refrigerate leftovers in an airtight container for up to 3 days.

NUTRITION · PER ONE SERVING

Calories **278 (13%)**
Total Fat **11.2 g (23%)**
  Saturated Fat **7.095 g**
  Polyunsaturated Fat **0.55 g**
  Monounsaturated Fat **2.932 g**
  Trans Fat **0.001 g**
Cholesterol **0 mg**
Sodium **45 mg (3%)**
Total Carbohydrate: **42.05 g (17%)**
  Dietary Fiber: **0.7 g (3%)**
  Total Sugars: **15.13 g**

Protein: **2.82 g (5%)**
Vitamin A **0.14 mcg**
Vitamin C **0.01 mcg**
Vitamin D **0.00 mcg**
Potassium **165 mg (4%)**
Calcium **35 mg (4%)**
Iron **2.95 mg (16%)**

MAIN DESSERTS

Maple Date Cake

Makes 10 Servings

PREP TIME: 35 minutes • **COOK TIME:** 50 minutes • **TOTAL TIME:** 1 hour 25 minutes
Level 3: Moderate

Dates are an ancient and nutritious fruit that grow on palm trees throughout the Mediterranean region. They remain a popular fruit today, commonly used in granola bars, snacks, cookies, and of course, cakes. One bite of this gluten-free cake is so addicting that one slice is never enough!

INGREDIENTS

2 cups dates, pitted and chopped

2 cups boiling water

4 large eggs

½ cup maple syrup

½ cup brown sugar, packed

¼ cup extra-virgin olive oil

1 teaspoon vanilla extract

¾ cup almond flour

¾ cup oat flour

1 teaspoon baking powder

1 teaspoon ground cinnamon

¼ teaspoon ground cardamom

¼ teaspoon allspice

¼ cup unsalted sunflower seeds

INSTRUCTIONS

1. Preheat oven to 350°F and coat an 8-×-8-inch baking dish with non-stick spray.

2. Place the chopped dates in a bowl and cover with boiling water. Set aside to soak for 10 minutes.

3. Drain the dates and place them in a food processor with the eggs, maple syrup, sugar, olive oil, and vanilla extract, and pulse until combined.

4. Add the almond flour, oat flour, baking powder, cinnamon, cardamom, and allspice, and pulse until just incorporated.

5. Spread the batter into the prepared baking dish and sprinkle with the sunflower seeds.

6. Bake for 40–50 minutes, until a skewer comes out clean.

7. Cool in the pan for 5–10 minutes, then transfer to a wire rack to cool completely.

8. Serve at room temperature. Refrigerate leftovers in an airtight container for up to 3 days.

NUTRITION · PER ONE SERVING

Calories **287 (13%)**
Total Fat **11.63 g (24%)**
  Saturated Fat **1.836 g**
  Polyunsaturated Fat **1.762 g**
  Monounsaturated Fat **7.501 g**
  Trans Fat **0.004 g**
Cholesterol **74 mg**
Sodium **45 mg (3%)**
Total Carbohydrate: **44.93 g (18%)**
  Dietary Fiber: **3.4 g (14%)**
  Total Sugars: **33.88 g**

Protein: **4.09 g (7%)**
Vitamin A **105 mcg (5%)**
Vitamin C **0.3 mcg**
Vitamin D **15 mcg (3%)**
Potassium **303 mg (6%)**
Calcium **87 mg (9%)**
Iron **192 mg (9%)**

Baked-Apple Baklava

Makes 4 servings

PREP TIME: 45 minutes • **COOK TIME:** 55 minutes • **TOTAL TIME:** 1 hour 40 minutes
Level 4: Challenging

Traditionally, baklava is a layered dessert with pastry, nuts, and syrup. In this recipe, I use store-bought puff pastry for the phyllo, simplifying the extensive process. Here, sweet Honeycrisp apples are sprinkled with spiced sugar, stuffed with honeyed nuts, and roasted to perfection, adding a fruity flourish to a classic dessert.

INGREDIENTS

For the apples:

¼ cup pecans

¼ cup sunflower seeds

¼ cup honey

1 teaspoons ground cinnamon

½ teaspoon nutmeg

4 large Honeycrisp apples, cored

¼ cup butter, room temperature

For the baklava:

1¼ cups plain Greek yogurt

¼ cup honey

1 teaspoon vanilla extract

1 sheet puff pastry, thawed

2 tablespoons brown sugar

1 teaspoon ground cinnamon

INSTRUCTIONS

1. Preheat oven to 350°F.

To make the apples:

1. Combine pecans, sunflower seeds, honey, cinnamon, and nutmeg in a small bowl, mixing well.

2. Make 4 square sheets of aluminum foil, each large enough to wrap and cover one apple. Coat one side of each aluminum foil sheet with non-stick cooking spray.

3. Individually place cored apples onto a foil sheet. Fill each core ¼ of the way with the nut and spice mixture and a tablespoon of butter.

4. Tightly wrap each apple in foil and arrange standing up on a cookie sheet. Bake for 30–40 minutes. Remove from oven and allow to cool for 15 minutes.

To make the baklava:

1. Whisk together the yogurt, honey, and vanilla extract in a small bowl and refrigerate.

2. Lay the sheet of puff pastry on a lightly floured surface and cut into 12 triangles.

recipe and ingredients continue

⅛ teaspoon nutmeg

2 tablespoons butter, melted

3. Whisk together the brown sugar, cinnamon, and nutmeg in a separate small bowl.

4. Brush each pastry triangle with melted butter and sprinkle with the spiced sugar mixture.

5. Transfer the pastry triangles onto a parchment-lined cookie sheet. Once the apples are finished baking, remove from oven, and allow to cool. Bake the pastry triangles for 12–15 minutes, until golden brown.

6. Remove pastry triangles from oven and allow to cool for 10–15 minutes.

7. Gently unwrap each apple and place on a cutting board. Pour the juices into the serving dishes.

8. Cut each apple in half and arrange two halves in each dessert bowl and top with 3 puff pastry triangles.

9. Drizzle each dish with the honey yogurt sauce.

10. Serve warm. Refrigerate leftovers in an airtight container for up to 3 days.

NUTRITION · PER ONE SERVING

Calories **620 (28%)**
Total Fat **31.52 g (65%)**
 Saturated Fat **13.088 g**
 Polyunsaturated Fat **4.712 g**
 Monounsaturated Fat **11.234 g**
 Trans Fat **0.702 g**
Cholesterol **49 mg**
Sodium **197 mg (13%)**
Total Carbohydrate: **81.22 g (33%)**
 Dietary Fiber: **7.7 g (31%)**
 Total Sugars: **64.62 g**

Protein: **11.43 g (21%)**
Vitamin A **668 mcg (29%)**
Vitamin C **10.7 mcg (14%)**
Vitamin D **13 mcg (2%)**
Potassium **463 mg (10%)**
Calcium **125 mg (13%)**
Iron **1.54 mg (9%)**

Sardinian Almond Cake

Makes 8 servings

PREP TIME: 35 minutes • **COOK TIME:** 40 minutes • **TOTAL TIME:** 1 hour 15 minutes
Level 4: Challenging

Also known as Torta Di Mandorle, this cake is native to the Mediterranean island of Sardinia. Although it's usually served at teatime in Tuscany, it also Makes a satisfying close to dinner. The delicate lime glaze subtly enhances the flavor of this versatile cake.

INGREDIENTS

For the cake:

- 4 large eggs, separated
- ¼ teaspoon cream of tartar
- ¾ cup + 1 tablespoon granulated sugar, divided
- 1 teaspoon vanilla extract
- 1 cup almond flour
- 2 tablespoons tapioca starch
- Zest of 1 lime
- 1 teaspoon baking powder

For the glaze:

- 1¼ cups powdered sugar
- 2 tablespoons lime juice
- ½ cup slivered almonds

INSTRUCTIONS

To make the cake:

1. Preheat oven to 350°F. Coat a 9-inch Springform pan with nonstick spray.

2. Combine the egg whites and cream of tartar in the bowl of a stand mixer outfitted with a whisk attachment and whip on low for 1 minute, until foamy.

3. Increase the mixer speed to medium and gradually add ¼ cup of the sugar, beat for 5–6 minutes, until stiff peaks are formed.

4. Whisk together the egg yolks, vanilla extract, and the remaining granulated sugar in a large bowl, until pale yellow in color.

5. Whisk together the almond flour, tapioca starch, lime zest, and baking powder in a separate small bowl.

6. Add the almond flour mixture to the egg yolk mixture, stirring to combine.

7. Carefully fold in the beaten egg whites into the batter.

recipe continues

8. Pour the batter into the prepared pan and bake for 40 minutes, or until a skewer inserted near the center of the cake comes out clean.

9. Allow the cake to cool in the pan for 5–10 minutes, and then transfer to a wire rack to cool completely.

To make the glaze:

1. Whisk together the powdered sugar and lime juice in a small bowl, until thick and smooth.

2. Pour the glaze over the cooled cake and top with the slivered almonds.

3. Allow the lime glaze to set before transferring to a serving plate. Refrigerate leftovers in an airtight container for up to 3 days.

NUTRITION · PER ONE SERVING

Calories **290 (13%)**
Total Fat **11.59 g (24%)**
　Saturated Fat **1.521 g**
　Polyunsaturated Fat **2.656 g**
　Monounsaturated Fat **6.875 g**
　Trans Fat **0.003 g**
Cholesterol **92 mg**
Sodium **78 mg (5%)**
Total Carbohydrate: **41.93 g (17%)**
　Dietary Fiber: **2.4 g (10%)**
　Total Sugars: **35.27 g**

Protein: **7.13 g (13%)**
Vitamin A **128 mcg (5%)**
Vitamin C **2.8 mcg (4%)**
Vitamin D **19 mcg (3%)**
Potassium **202 mg (4%)**
Calcium **107 mg (11%)**
Iron **1.07 mg (4%)**

MAIN DESSERTS

Lemon Olive Oil Pound Cake

Makes 8 servings

PREP TIME: 45 minutes • **COOK TIME:** 45 minutes • **TOTAL TIME:** 1 hour 30 minutes
Level 3: Moderate

Trust me when I say that this scrumptious pound cake featuring lemons, olive oil, and mascarpone cheese is no ordinary pound cake. For one, it is light and fluffy, and two, the cheese and oil contain healthy fats. But just like all pound cakes, it always hits the spot.

INGREDIENTS

For the pound cake:

- ¾ cup granulated sugar
- 2 large eggs, separated
- 1 cup all-purpose flour
- Zest of 2 lemons
- 1 teaspoon baking powder
- ¼ teaspoon sea salt
- ¼ teaspoon cream of tartar
- ¾ cup mascarpone cheese
- ⅓ cup extra-virgin olive oil
- ¼ cup lemon juice, freshly squeezed
- 1½ tablespoons whole milk
- 1 teaspoon vanilla extract
- 1 teaspoon almond extract
- 3½ tablespoons unsalted butter, melted

INSTRUCTIONS

To make the cake:

1. Preheat oven to 325°F and coat a 9-×-5-inch loaf pan with non-stick spray.

2. Whisk together the sugar and egg yolks in a large bowl for 3–4 minutes, until thick, pale, and foamy.

3. Whisk together the flour, lemon zest, baking powder, and salt in a separate medium bowl.

4. Add the dry Ingredients to the wet Ingredients, and whisk until combined.

5. Combine the egg whites and cream of tartar in the bowl of a stand mixer outfitted with a whisk attachment and whip on low for 1 minute, until foamy. Increase the mixer speed to medium and beat for 5–6 minutes, until stiff peaks form.

6. Whisk together the mascarpone cheese, olive oil, lemon juice, milk, vanilla extract, and almond extract in a separate medium bowl, until combined.

7. Add the mascarpone cheese mixture to the egg yolk and flour mixture, mixing just until incorporated. Add the butter and mix to combine.

8. Carefully fold the beaten egg whites into the batter.

For the topping:

1 cup powdered sugar

9. Pour batter into the prepared loaf pan and bake for 40–45 minutes, until golden brown.

10. Allow cake to cool in the pan for 5–10 minutes, then transfer to a wire rack to cool completely.

Adding the topping:

1. Pour the sugar into a fine strainer. Hold the strainer over the cake and then gently shake out the sugar onto the cake until it's evenly covered with a fine layer of sugar. Serve and enjoy! Refrigerate leftovers in an airtight container for up to 3 days.

NUTRITION • PER ONE SERVING

Calories **269 (12%)**
Total Fat **11.58 g (24%)**
  Saturated Fat **4.613 g**
  Polyunsaturated Fat **0.908 g**
  Monounsaturated Fat **5.08 g**
  Trans Fat **0.1 g**
Cholesterol **64 mg**
Sodium **301 mg (20%)**
Total Carbohydrate: **36.23 g (15%)**
  Dietary Fiber: **0.5 g (2%)**
  Total Sugars: **22.57 g**

Protein: **5.7 g (10%)**
Vitamin A **271 mcg (12%)**
Vitamin C **8.7 mcg (12%)**
Vitamin D **26 mcg (4%)**
Potassium **86 mg (2%)**
Calcium **124 mg (12%)**
Iron **1.04 mg (6%)**

Revani Cake (Basbousa)

Makes 16 servings

PREP TIME: 20 minutes • **COOK TIME:** 35 minutes • **TOTAL TIME:** 3 hours 55 minutes
Level 3: Moderate

This traditional semolina cake is soaked in a simple syrup which elevates it from an everyday dessert to one also suited for special occasions. Originating in Egypt, this version is sprinkled with shredded coconut, which always brings out the best in any lemon cake. To follow in centuries of tradition, serve this dessert cut into squares.

INGREDIENTS

For the syrup:

1½ cups water

½ cup honey

½ cup brown sugar, packed

½ cup granulated sugar

Juice of one lemon

1 teaspoon vanilla extract

For the cake:

4 large eggs, room temperature

¼ cup granulated sugar

¼ cup brown sugar, packed

¼ cup butter, melted

1 teaspoon vanilla extract

1 teaspoon almond extract

1 teaspoon lemon extract

¾ cup all-purpose flour

INSTRUCTIONS

1. Preheat oven to 350°F and line a 9-×-9-inch cake pan with parchment paper.

To make the syrup:

1. Whisk together the water, honey, both sugars, lemon juice, and vanilla extract in a saucepan.

2. Place over medium-high heat for 5 minutes, until the sugar crystals dissolve. Remove from heat and cool completely.

To make the cake:

1. Combine the eggs and both sugars in the bowl of a stand mixer outfitted with the whisk attachment. Whip mixture on high for 4–5 minutes, until it increases in volume, is fluffy and pale yellow in color.

2. Add the melted butter, vanilla extract, almond extract, and lemon extract and continue beating until combined.

3. Whisk together the all-purpose flour, semolina, baking powder, and salt in a separate bowl.

4. Gradually add the flour mixture to the standing mixer's bowl. Beat on low speed, until combined.

¾ cup finely ground semolina flour

1 teaspoon baking powder

¼ teaspoon salt

½ cup sweetened coconut, shredded and toasted

½ cup walnuts, finely chopped

5. Pour the cake batter into the prepared pan and bake for 25–30 minutes, until a skewer comes out clean.

6. Remove pan to a rack and immediately poke holes into the hot cake with a skewer, then pour the syrup over it.

7. Cool cake for 2–3 hours and then transfer to a serving dish.

8. Top with the toasted coconut and walnuts, and serve. Refrigerate leftovers in an airtight container for up to 3 days.

NUTRITION · PER ONE SERVING

Calories **265 (12%)**
Total Fat **9.91 g (20%)**
  Saturated Fat **5.432 g**
  Polyunsaturated Fat **2.116 g**
  Monounsaturated Fat **1.752 g**
  Trans Fat **0.116 g**
Cholesterol **54 mg**
Sodium **91 mg (3%)**
Total Carbohydrate: **42.58 g (17%)**
  Dietary Fiber: **0.7 g (3%)**
  Total Sugars: **28.35 g**

Protein: **3.31 g (6%)**
Vitamin A **151 mcg (6%)**
Vitamin C **1.5 mcg (2%)**
Vitamin D **11 mcg (2%)**
Potassium **106 mg (2%)**
Calcium **47 mg (5%)**
Iron **0.99 mg (6%)**

Spanish Almond Cookies (Almendrados)

Makes 18 cookies

PREP TIME: 30 minutes • **COOK TIME:** 15 minutes • **TOTAL TIME:** 45 minutes
Level 3: Moderate

Almonds have been used for centuries in Spanish desserts. These melt-in-your-mouth cookies make the best of that tradition by using almond flour to create an irresistibly tender, crumbly, and gluten-free cookie. Typically served during the Christmas season, they'll be a welcome addition to your cookie tray.

INGREDIENTS

- 10 tablespoons butter
- 1 cup granulated sugar
- 1 cup blanched almond flour, packed
- ½ cup oat flour
- ¼ cup sorghum flour
- 1 teaspoon ground cinnamon
- ¼ teaspoon fine sea salt
- ⅛ teaspoon star anise powder

INSTRUCTIONS

1. Preheat oven to 350°F and line two cookie sheets with parchment paper.

2. Place the sugar and butter into the bowl of a stand mixer outfitted with the paddle attachment and mix on medium speed for 30–60 seconds, until the consistency resembles large crumbs.

3. Whisk together the almond flour, oat flour, sorghum flour, cinnamon, salt, and star anise in a separate medium bowl.

4. Slowly add the flour mixture to the butter mixture and mix on low speed for 3–4 minutes, until a shaggy dough forms.

5. Turn dough onto a sheet of parchment paper and lightly sprinkle with oat flour.

6. Form the cookie dough into a ball in center of the floured parchment paper and flatten slightly with your hand.

7. Top with another piece of parchment paper and roll out the dough to a thickness of ½-inch.

recipe continues

8. Use a 2-inch-round cutter to form the cookies and carefully transfer them to the prepared sheets, leaving 2-inches of space between each cookie. Reroll scraps of dough to cut additional cookies.

9. Bake for 13–15 minutes, until slightly golden.

10. Allow cookies to cool for 5 minutes and then transfer to a wire rack to cool completely. Serve and enjoy! Refrigerate leftovers in an airtight container for up to 3 days.

NUTRITION · PER ONE SERVING

Calories **127 (6%)**
Total Fat **9.36 g (19%)**
  Saturated Fat **4.309 g**
  Polyunsaturated Fat **1.011 g**
  Monounsaturated Fat **3.424 g**
  Trans Fat **0.259 g**
Cholesterol **17 mg**
Sodium **84 mg (6%)**
Total Carbohydrate: **10 g (4%)**
  Dietary Fiber: **1 g (4%)**
  Total Sugars: **1.25 g**

Protein: **1.76 g (3%)**
Vitamin A **198 mcg (8%)**
Vitamin C **0 mcg**
Vitamin D **5 mcg (1%)**
Potassium **58 mg (1%)**
Calcium **20 mg (2%)**
Iron **0.39 mg (2%)**

Peach Crumb Tart

Makes 8 servings

PREP TIME: 40 minutes • **COOK TIME:** 1 hour • **TOTAL TIME:** 1 hour 40 minutes
Level 3: Moderate

This Peach Crumb Tart leaves nothing to be desired—it has it all—flaky crust, fresh sweet peaches, and a crunchy crumb topping. Extremely popular in countless Mediterranean desserts, peaches elevate this recipe as the juices magically evolve into a heavenly syrup. No summer menu is complete without this antioxidant-rich dessert.

INGREDIENTS

For the filling:

4 peaches, thinly sliced

3 tablespoons brown sugar

2 tablespoons all-purpose flour

Juice of 1 lemon

1 teaspoon ground cinnamon

For the dough:

1¼ cups all-purpose flour

½ cup granulated sugar

½ cup brown sugar

1 teaspoon ground cinnamon

½ teaspoon ground cardamom

½ teaspoon sea salt

¼ teaspoon baking powder

½ cup unsalted butter, chilled and cubed

1 tablespoon water

INSTRUCTIONS

1. Preheat oven to 350°F and lightly coat a 9-inch tart pan with non-stick cooking spray.

To make the filling:

1. Combine all the filling Ingredients in a medium bowl, tossing to combine.

To make the dough:

1. Whisk together the flour, granulated sugar, brown sugar, cinnamon, cardamom, salt, and baking powder in a large bowl.

2. Rub with your fingers or use a pastry cutter to incorporate the butter cubes until it resembles coarse crumbs. Set aside ¾ of the mixture.

3. To the remaining crumb mixture, add the water, vanilla extract, and almond extract, mixing until it combines enough to press into the bottom of the prepared pan. Top the crust with the peach filling.

4. Sprinkle the reserved crumb topping over the tart, then top with the pecans. Bake for 1 hour, rotating after 30 minutes.

recipe and ingredients continue

1 teaspoon vanilla extract

½ teaspoon almond extract

¼ cup pecans, finely chopped

2 tablespoons powdered sugar

5. Cool in the pan for 15–20 minutes. Once cool enough to handle, remove tart from the pan, and transfer to a wire rack to cool completely.

6. Sprinkle the powdered sugar over top and serve at room temperature. Top with ice cream or whipped cream, if desired. Refrigerate leftovers in an airtight container for up to 3 days.

NUTRITION · PER ONE SERVING

Calories **250 (11%)**
Total Fat **10.23 g (21%)**
  Saturated Fat **5.039 g**
  Polyunsaturated Fat **1.062 g**
  Monounsaturated Fat **3.544 g**
  Trans Fat **0 g**
Cholesterol **15 mg**
Sodium **164 mg (11%)**
Total Carbohydrate: **37.29 g (15%)**
  Dietary Fiber: **1.4 g (6%)**
  Total Sugars: **19.25 g**

Protein: **3.09 g (6%)**
Vitamin A **264 mcg (11%)**
Vitamin C **9.7 mcg (13%)**
Vitamin D **6 mcg (1%)**
Potassium **68 mg (1%)**
Calcium **31 mg (3%)**
Iron **1.37 mg (8%)**

Loukoumades (Greek Honey Balls)

Makes 40 servings

PREP TIME: 20 minutes • **COOK TIME:** 20 minutes • **TOTAL TIME:** 1 hour 35 minutes
Level 4: Challenging

Also known as fried Greek donuts, these Honey Balls are an irresistible treat thanks to their fluffy texture and crunchy coating of chopped pecans and honey. They are also dairy-free, but if you don't need to worry about lactose, serve with ice cream or a dollop of whipped cream for an instant crowd pleaser.

INGREDIENTS

For the dough:

2 cups lukewarm water, divided

1 teaspoon active dry yeast

3 cups + 2 tablespoons all-purpose flour

2 tablespoons granulated sugar

1 teaspoon salt

1 teaspoon cinnamon

For frying:

4 cups vegetable oil

1 cup water

For the topping:

¼ cup powdered sugar

¼ cup pecans, roughly chopped

1 tablespoon cinnamon

1 teaspoon nutmeg

¼ cup honey

INSTRUCTIONS

To make the dough:

1. Whisk ¼ cup of the water with the yeast in a large bowl and allow to sit for 5 minutes, until foamy.

2. Add the flour, sugar, salt, cinnamon, and remaining water to the bowl, mixing until a dough forms.

3. Cover bowl with plastic wrap and let rest in a warm area for 45–55 minutes, until it triples in size.

To fry:

1. Heat the oil in a 6-quart soup pot set over medium-high heat, until it reaches 350°F.

2. Wet hands to keep the dough from sticking, take approximately two tablespoons (a small handful) of the dough, and roll into balls. Carefully drop into the hot oil. You will have to work in batches, so the balls do not stick together.

3. Cook balls for 1–2 minutes per side, until golden brown.

4. Remove from the hot oil and drain on a wire rack set over a rimmed cookie sheet, and start the next batch.

To make the topping:

1. Whisk together the powdered sugar, pecans, cinnamon, and nutmeg in a small bowl.

2. Once cooled, coat balls with honey and sprinkle with the mixture (optional). Serve warm or at room temperature. Refrigerate leftovers in an airtight container for up to 3 days.

NUTRITION • PER ONE SERVING

Calories **247 (11%)**	Protein: **1.09 g (2%)**
Total Fat **22.37 g (46%)**	Vitamin A **1 mcg**
Saturated Fat **3.481 g**	Vitamin C **0 mcg**
Polyunsaturated Fat **12.76 g**	Vitamin D **0 mcg**
Monounsaturated Fat **5.235 g**	Potassium **16 mg**
Trans Fat **0.116 g**	Calcium **7 mg (1%)**
Cholesterol **0 mg**	Iron **0.5 mg (3%)**
Sodium **59 mg (4%)**	
Total Carbohydrate: **10.51 g (4%)**	
Dietary Fiber: **0.5 g (2%)**	
Total Sugars: **3.03 g**	

MAIN DESSERTS

Mediterranean Rice Pudding

Makes 4 servings

PREP TIME: 15 minutes • **COOK TIME:** 35 minutes • **TOTAL TIME:** 50 minutes
Level 3: Moderate

Rice pudding is a heavenly treat no matter in which country it's served. In the Mediterranean, it's flavored with spices and a hint of citrus, making this creamy dish the perfect dessert whether you're at a fancy dinner or an informal gathering. This particular version is inspired by the Greek dessert Rizogalo (rizi = rice, gala = milk)!

INGREDIENTS

2 cups whole milk

1 2-inch cinnamon stick

1 star anise

1 tablespoon lemon zest

1 tablespoon orange zest

½ cup short-grain rice

⅓ cup granulated sugar

1 teaspoon butter

1 teaspoon ground cinnamon

INSTRUCTIONS

1. Combine the milk, cinnamon stick, star anise, lemon zest, and orange zest in saucepan set over medium-high heat, until bubbles form around the edge of the pan.

2. Rinse the short-grain rice in a sieve under running water to remove some of the starch.

3. Add the rice to the hot milk and simmer for 10 minutes.

4. Remove the cinnamon stick and star anise from hot rice pudding, turn heat to low, and cook an additional 10–15 minutes, until the rice is tender.

5. Remove pudding from heat, add the sugar and butter, stirring until the sugar dissolves.

6. Divide the hot pudding evenly into 4 dessert bowls and sprinkle each with ground cinnamon.

7. Cover each pudding with plastic wrap and press directly against the pudding's surface to prevent a film from forming and allow to cool.

8. Serve warm or at room temperature and enjoy! Refrigerate leftovers in an airtight container for up to 3 days.

NUTRITION · PER ONE SERVING

Calories **216 (10%)**
Total Fat **5.37 g (11%)**
   Saturated Fat **2.93 g**
   Polyunsaturated Fat **0.364 g**
   Monounsaturated Fat **1.446 g**
   Trans Fat **0.039 g**
Cholesterol **15 mg**
Sodium **61 mg (4%)**
Total Carbohydrate: **36.45 g (15%)**
   Dietary Fiber: **1.7 g (7%)**
Total Sugars: **14.68 g**

Protein: **5.86 g (11%)**
Vitamin A **238 mcg (18%)**
Vitamin C **3.2 mcg (4%)**
Vitamin D **3 mcg (1%)**
Potassium **221 mg (5%)**
Calcium **163 mg (16%)**
Iron **1.83 mg (10%)**

Olive Oil Cornmeal Cookies

Makes 12 servings

PREP TIME: 35 minutes • **COOK TIME:** 13 minutes • **TOTAL TIME:** 48 minutes
Level 3: Moderate

Serve these cookies with ice wine for the perfect after-dinner treat. The flavor of these cookies depends on the quality of the olive oil, so choose the best and make sure the taste is light, fresh, and fruity, not heavy or bitter. You'll be surprised at how well the sweetness of the cookie compliments the sharper, almost minty flavor of the thyme!

INGREDIENTS

¾ cup all-purpose flour

¼ cup cornmeal

½ teaspoon baking powder

½ teaspoon ground cinnamon

⅛ teaspoon salt

⅓ cup extra-virgin olive oil

¼ cup brown sugar, packed

1 large egg

½ teaspoon fresh thyme leaves, minced

⅓ cup powdered sugar

INSTRUCTIONS

1. Move oven rack to the center of the oven and preheat to 375ºF, then line a cookie sheet with a parchment sheet.

2. Whisk together the flour, cornmeal, baking powder, cinnamon, and salt in a small bowl.

3. Whisk together the olive oil and brown sugar in a separate large bowl. Add the egg and thyme, whisking until incorporated.

4. Fold the flour cornmeal mixture into the olive oil mixture, mixing until a soft dough forms.

5. Scoop dough in tablespoons onto the prepared cookie sheet leaving 2-inches of space between each cookie.

6. Bake for 12–13 minutes. Cool cookies for 10 minutes on the pan.

7. Roll the warm cookies in the powdered sugar and place on a wire rack to cool completely before serving. Refrigerate leftovers in an airtight container for up to 3 days.

NUTRITION · PER ONE SERVING

Calories **127 (6%)**
Total Fat **6.48 g (13%)**
  Saturated Fat **0.971 g**
  Polyunsaturated Fat **0.765 g**
  Monounsaturated Fat **4.505 g**
  Trans Fat **0.004 g**
Cholesterol **16 mg**
Sodium **86 mg (6%)**
Total Carbohydrate: **15.93 g (6%)**
  Dietary Fiber: **0.4 g (2%)**
  Total Sugars: **2.44 g**

Protein: **1.57 g (3%)**
Vitamin A **31 mcg (1%)**
Vitamin C **0 mcg**
Vitamin D **3 mcg (1%)**
Potassium **26 mg (1%)**
Calcium **9 mg (1%)**
Iron **0.55 mg (3%)**

Maple Orange Phyllo with Spiced Fruit

Makes 4 servings

PREP TIME: 30 minutes • **COOK TIME:** 13 minutes • **TOTAL TIME:** 1 hour 43 minutes
Level 4: Challenging

Take crispy, flaky phyllo squares, smeared with sweetened Greek yogurt, topped with marinated spiced, citrus dates and nuts, and you're in dessert nirvana. Serve this to your loved ones and I guarantee they'll beg for it to be added to your weekly repertoire. Rich in fruit and almonds, you'll also be serving up a vitamin-rich treat.

INGREDIENTS

For the dough:

6 sheets phyllo dough, thawed

¼ cup brown sugar

¼ teaspoon ground cinnamon

⅛ teaspoon nutmeg

¼ cup unsalted butter, melted

For the spiced fruit:

2 tablespoons granulated sugar

2 tablespoons maple syrup

Zest of 1 orange

Juice of 1 orange

½ cup dried cranberries, roughly chopped

1 cup unsalted almonds, roasted and roughly chopped

INSTRUCTIONS

1. Preheat oven to 400°F and line a cookie sheet with parchment paper.

To make the dough:

1. Cover the thawed phyllo dough with a damp cloth and set aside.

2. Whisk together the brown sugar, cinnamon, and nutmeg in a small bowl.

3. Place 1 sheet of phyllo dough onto the prepared cookie sheet, brush it with melted butter and sprinkle with the cinnamon-sugar mixture. Cover with another sheet of phyllo and repeat for every sheet of phyllo, ending with a coating of butter and cinnamon-sugar.

4. Cut the layered phyllo into 12 squares using kitchen shears.

5. Bake for 7–8 minutes, until golden brown and crisp. Remove from oven and cool completely on the pan.

recipe and ingredients continue

½ cup dates, pitted and roughly chopped

¼ teaspoon cinnamon

¼ teaspoon ginger

For the sauce:

1 cup whole milk Greek yogurt

1 tablespoon maple syrup

Zest of 1 lemon

For the garnish:

½ cup pomegranate seeds

¼ cup almonds, chopped

¼ cup raspberries

¼ cup strawberries

2 tablespoons maple syrup

To make the spiced fruit:

1. Combine the sugar, maple syrup, orange zest and juice in a saucepot set over medium heat for 3–5 minutes, until the sugar dissolves. Remove from heat and stir in the cranberries.

2. Combine the almonds, dates, cinnamon, and ginger in a bowl and add to the orange syrup. Stir and set aside to marinate for 1 hour at room temperature.

To make the sauce:

1. Whisk together the yogurt, maple syrup, and lemon zest in a small bowl until smooth.

2. Spread 1 tablespoon of the yogurt sauce on each of four phyllo squares and place each on an individual serving plate. Add a spoonful of the nut-fruit mixture to each and top with another phyllo square. Repeat until each plate contains three phyllo squares.

To garnish:

1. Before serving, top with pomegranate seeds, almonds, raspberries, strawberries, maple syrup or any other glaze of your choice. Refrigerate leftovers in an airtight container for up to 3 days.

NUTRITION · PER ONE SERVING

Calories **2667 (122%)**
Total Fat **135.16 g (278%)**
  Saturated Fat **32.993 g**
  Polyunsaturated Fat **24.051 g**
  Monounsaturated Fat **69.682 g**
  Trans Fat **0 g**
Cholesterol **91 mg**
Sodium **710 mg (47%)**
Total Carbohydrate: **338.6 g (138%)**
  Dietary Fiber: **34.8 g (139%)**
  Total Sugars: **223.27 g**

Protein: **57.75 g (106%)**
Vitamin A **43.77 mcg (62%)**
Vitamin C **166 mcg (221%)**
Vitamin D **27 mcg (5%)**
Potassium **3008 mg (64%)**
Calcium **992 mg (99%)**
Iron **12.42 mg (69%)**

Crème Brûlée

Makes 8 servings

PREP TIME: 35 minutes • **COOK TIME:** 55 minutes • **TOTAL TIME:** 5 hours 30 minutes
Level 4: Challenging

Crème Brûlée is a French dessert with a pedigree dating back to 1691. Its name literally translates to burnt cream. This Mediterranean-inspired version infuses the rich and creamy custard with lavender and clove. What Makes this dessert so special is its sugar topping, torched to crackling perfection.

INGREDIENTS

2½ cups whipping cream, room temperature

1 tablespoon whole cloves

1 tablespoon vanilla extract

1 tablespoon lavender extract

10 large egg yolks, room temperature

¾ cup granulated sugar, divided

INSTRUCTIONS

1. Preheat oven to 300°F. Construct a Bain Marie to cook the custard by arranging 8 (6-oz.) ramekins in a roasting or baking pan just large enough to hold them.* Set a kettle with at least 3 cups of water to boil.

2. Combine the whipping cream and cloves in a medium saucepan set over medium-low heat, cooking for 4–5 minutes, until just hot. Remove pan from heat and let sit for 3–4 minutes, and then discard the cloves.

3. Stir in the vanilla and lavender extracts.

4. Whisk together the egg yolks and ½ cup of the sugar in a medium bowl until pale yellow in color and the sugar is dissolved.

5. Add a ladle of the hot cream mixture to the eggs and whisk to temper the eggs so they don't curdle.

6. Gradually add the warmed egg mixture to the pot containing the cream while whisking constantly, until combined.

recipe continues

NOTES: *Do not use a Dutch Oven or other deep pot, as the sides will retain too much heat and ruin the custard.

**If you do not have a torch, arrange the sugar-topped ramekins at least 2–3 inches from the heat under the broiler on low for 5 minutes (while watching carefully), until the sugar melts and the slightly burnt caramel forms.

7. Ladle the mixture into the arranged ramekins, leaving ¼-inch of headspace.

8. Carefully add the boiling water to the pan, reaching halfway up the sides of the ramekins. Be careful not to get water in the ramekins. Bake in the water bath for 50 minutes, until custard is set.

9. Carefully remove the Bain Marie from the oven and allow the custards to cool in the water.

10. Once cool, remove ramekins from the water bath, dry the bottom of each, and place them in the fridge to chill for 2–4 hours.

11. Before serving, sprinkle the remaining sugar over the top of each Crème Brûlée and use a torch to melt the sugar and form a slightly burnt caramel crust.**

12. Before serving, return the ramekins to the refrigerator for 5 minutes, allowing the caramel to harden. Refrigerate leftovers in an airtight container for up to 3 days.

NUTRITION · PER ONE SERVING

Calories **409 (19%)**
Total Fat **33.23 g (68%)**
  Saturated Fat **19.179 g**
  Polyunsaturated Fat **1.933 g**
  Monounsaturated Fat **10.447 g**
  Trans Fat **0 g**
Cholesterol **322 mg**
Sodium **40 mg (3%)**
Total Carbohydrate: **22.54 g (9%)**
  Dietary Fiber: **0.2 g (1%)**
  Total Sugars: **21.32 g**

Protein: **4.94 g (9%)**
Vitamin A **1404 mcg (60%)**
Vitamin C **0.7 mcg (1%)**
Vitamin D **66 mcg (11%)**
Potassium **92 mg (2%)**
Calcium **81 mg (8%)**
Iron **0.67 mg (4%)**

Toasted Coconut Cornmeal Cake

Makes 8 servings

PREP TIME: 30 minutes • **COOK TIME:** 50 minutes • **TOTAL TIME:** 1 hr 20 minutes
Level 3: Moderate

Toasted coconut is the star of this cake. Paired with cinnamon, olive oil, and a splash of Chardonnay, this cake is bursting with unparalleled flavor. This versatile cake can be served for breakfast with fruit (fresh oranges work especially well) and whipped cream, or as an afternoon snack with coffee or tea. This cake is guaranteed to sweeten your day!

INGREDIENTS

1 cup sweetened coconut, shredded

1 cup granulated sugar

2 large eggs

½ cup extra-virgin olive oil

½ cup Chardonnay

1¼ cups all-purpose flour

½ cup fine cornmeal

2 teaspoons baking powder

1 teaspoon salt

½ teaspoon ground cinnamon

Zest of 1 lemon

3 tablespoons powdered sugar

INSTRUCTIONS

1. Preheat oven to 350°F and line a cookie sheet with parchment paper.

2. Spread the coconut on the cookie sheet in an even layer and bake for 8–10 minutes, stirring every two minutes, until it is evenly golden brown. Remove from oven and allow to cool completely on the pan.

3. Turn oven to 375°F and line an 8-inch cake pan with parchment paper.

4. Whisk together the sugar, eggs, olive oil, and Chardonnay in a large bowl, until smooth.

5. Combine the flour, cornmeal, baking powder, salt, cinnamon, and lemon zest in a separate medium bowl, whisking well before adding to wet Ingredients. Stir just until incorporated.

6. Gently fold in the toasted coconut and pour the batter into the prepared pan. Bake for 35–40 minutes, until a skewer comes out clean. Allow the cake to cool in the pan for 20 minutes.

7. Carefully remove the cake from the pan and peel off the parchment paper. Place the cake on a wire rack to cool completely.

8. Before serving, dust with powdered sugar. Refrigerate leftovers in an airtight container for up to 3 days.

NUTRITION · PER ONE SERVING

Calories **425 (19%)**
Total Fat **19.19 g (40%)**
  Saturated Fat **5.968 g**
  Polyunsaturated Fat **1.868 g**
  Monounsaturated Fat **10.539 g**
  Trans Fat **0.011 g**
Cholesterol **47 mg**
Sodium **656 mg (44%)**
Total Carbohydrate: **57.19 g (23%)**
  Dietary Fiber: **1.5 g (6%)**
Total Sugars: **33.46 g**

Protein: **4.66 g (9%)**
Vitamin A **89 mcg (4%)**
Vitamin C **2.4 mcg (3%)**
Vitamin D **10 mcg (2%)**
Potassium **109 mg (2%)**
Calcium **16 mg (2%)**
Iron **1.61 mg (9%)**

Spiced Red Wine Cookies

Makes 32–36 cookies

PREP TIME: 35 minutes • **COOK TIME:** 30 minutes • **TOTAL TIME:** 1 hour 5 minutes
Level 4: Challenging

Featuring the bold flavors of cardamom, cloves, grapefruit, and red wine, this recipe will reset your cookie expectations. If the saying 'a glass of wine a day keeps the doctor away' is true, then these cookies may just do the trick thanks to the plentiful antioxidants in red wine!

INGREDIENTS

- 6 tablespoons extra-virgin olive oil
- 2½ tablespoons granulated sugar
- ⅓ cup + 3 tablespoons red wine
- 2½ tablespoons grapefruit juice
- 2½ tablespoons sesame seeds, roasted
- 1 teaspoon ground cardamom
- ½ teaspoon ground cinnamon
- ½ teaspoon ground cloves
- ½ tablespoon grapefruit zest
- ½ tablespoon baking powder
- 3–4 cups pastry flour
- ⅓ teaspoon baking soda
- 2½ cups brown sugar or 2½ cups of sesame seeds

INSTRUCTIONS

1. Preheat oven to 325°F and line 2 cookie sheets with parchment paper.

2. Whisk together the olive oil and granulated sugar in a medium bowl, then add the red wine, grapefruit juice, and sesame seeds, mixing well.

3. Add the cardamom, cinnamon, cloves, grapefruit zest, and baking powder, whisking until well blended.

4. Whisk together the flour and baking soda in a medium bowl then add half to the wet Ingredients and mix well.

5. Add the remaining flour mixture gradually, mixing as you go, until a dough forms (you may not need it all).

6. Knead the dough until smooth, but not sticky, and divide it into 4 equal portions (1 per cookie sheet). Set aside two portions.

7. Place one portion of the dough at a time onto a lightly floured surface and roll to a thickness of ½-inch. Using a cutter with any shape of your choice and dipped in flour, cut out the cookies, and arrange them on the two prepared cookie sheets. Sprinkle them with brown sugar or sesame seeds and bake for 25–30 minutes, until the edges have set.

8. Allow to cool on the cookie sheet for 5 minutes then transfer to a wire rack to cool completely.

9. Once the 2 prepared cookie sheets are cleared, keep the parchment paper on and repeat steps 7–8 for the remaining two dough portions.

10. Serve and enjoy! Refrigerate leftovers in an airtight container for up to 3 days.

NUTRITION • PER ONE SERVING

Calories **112 (5%)**
Total Fat **5.98 g (12%)**
   Saturated Fat **0.834 g**
   Polyunsaturated Fat **0.809 g**
   Monounsaturated Fat **4.123 g**
   Trans Fat **0.003 g**
Cholesterol **0 mg**
Sodium **26 mg (2%)**
Total Carbohydrate: **12.99 g (5%)**
   Dietary Fiber: **0.2 g (2%)**
   Total Sugars: **1.79 g**

Protein: **1.65 g (3%)**
Vitamin A **6 mcg (0%)**
Vitamin C **0.5 mcg (1%)**
Vitamin D **0 mcg**
Potassium **25 mg (1%)**
Calcium **19 mg (2%)**
Iron **0.79 mg (4%)**

MAIN DESSERTS

Tahini Brownies

Makes 16 servings

PREP TIME: 20 minutes • **COOK TIME:** 35 minutes • **TOTAL TIME:** 1 hour 20 minutes
Level 3: Moderate

Made from toasted and ground sesame seeds, tahini is naturally rich in omega-3 fatty acids and anti-inflammatory properties, making this dessert as healthy as it is delicious. The nutty flavor imparted by the tahini pairs perfectly with the chocolate, and the texture is moist, yet fudgy—truly the best of both worlds.

INGREDIENTS

¼ cup salted butter

¼ cup bittersweet chocolate chips

3 tablespoons cocoa powder

1 cup granulated sugar

2 large eggs

1 tablespoon vanilla extract

1 teaspoon kosher salt

¾ cup tahini

⅓ cup all-purpose flour

1 teaspoon espresso powder

¼ teaspoon ground cardamom

INSTRUCTIONS

1. Preheat oven to 350°F and line an 8-×-8-inch pan with 2 sheets of foil, making sure the excess foil hangs over the sides. Lightly coat foil with non-stick spray.

2. Heat the butter in a small saucepan set over low heat, until melted. Remove from heat and add the chocolate chips and cocoa powder, whisking until smooth. Set aside.

3. Whisk together the sugar, eggs, vanilla extract, and salt in a large bowl, until slightly thick.

4. Add the tahini, mixing until combined.

5. Whisk together the flour, espresso powder, and cardamom in a separate small bowl, then fold carefully into the wet Ingredients.

6. Remove half the tahini mixture to a separate bowl and set aside.

7. Add the warm chocolate butter mixture into one of the bowls with the tahini mixture, stirring until combined. Pour batter into the prepared pan and spread evenly.

recipe continues

8. Drop spoonfuls of the reserved tahini mixture onto the brownie batter 1-inch apart.

9. Using the tip of a paring knife or using a skewer, swirl the dollops of tahini mixture into the brownie batter, forming a marbling effect.

10. Bake the brownies for 28–30 minutes, until firm around the edges and a skewer comes out clean.

11. Cool in the pan for 25–30 minutes, then using the excess foil, carefully lift the brownies from the pan, and place on a wire rack to cool completely.

12. When cool, remove from the foil, cut into 16 squares, and serve. Refrigerate leftovers in an airtight container for up to 3 days.

NUTRITION · PER ONE SERVING

Calories **172 (8%)**
Total Fat **11.71 g (24%)**
  Saturated Fat **4.062 g**
  Polyunsaturated Fat **2.916 g**
  Monounsaturated Fat **4.04 g**
  Trans Fat **0.002 g**
Cholesterol **25 mg**
Sodium **177 mg (12%)**
Total Carbohydrate: **14.75 g (6%)**
  Dietary Fiber: **2.2 g (9%)**
  Total Sugars: **8.02 g**

Protein: **3.29 g (6%)**
Vitamin A **100 mcg (4%)**
Vitamin C **0 mcg**
Vitamin D **6 mcg (1%)**
Potassium **132 mg (3%)**
Calcium **59 mg (6%)**
Iron **2.21 mg (12%)**

Greek Bougatsa with Honey & Pistachios

Makes 10 servings

PREP TIME: 45 minutes • **COOK TIME:** 1 hour • **TOTAL TIME:** 1 hour 45 minutes
Level 3: Moderate

Constantinople (modern-day Istanbul) was under Greek rule before it was conquered by the Ottoman Empire in 1453. During that time, phyllo pastry was invented. Bougatsa is a traditional Greek custard pie made with phyllo. My version features a delicious vanilla pistachio custard encased in flaky phyllo.

INGREDIENTS

- 1 cup unsalted butter, melted and divided
- 2 sheets phyllo dough, thawed
- 2 vanilla beans
- 2¾ cups heavy cream
- 5 large eggs
- ¾ cup granulated sugar
- ¼ cup pistachio butter
- 3 teaspoons ground cinnamon, divided
- 3 tablespoons honey
- ¼ cup pistachios, chopped

INSTRUCTIONS

1. Preheat oven to 350°F and coat a 12-inch cake pan with a bit of the melted butter.

2. Separate the phyllo sheets and roll them into logs, place the first one in the center of the prepared pan, and arrange the rest around it until the bottom of the pan is covered.

3. Brush the logs with the melted butter, making sure to get it into every crevice.

4. Bake for 30 minutes, until logs are a golden brown.

5. While the pastry is baking, split the vanilla beans in half, remove the seeds, and place them in a large bowl.

6. Add the heavy cream, eggs, sugar, pistachio butter, and 1 teaspoon of the cinnamon. Whisk until smooth.

recipe continues

7. Pour the custard mixture over the hot logs and bake for an additional 20–30 minutes, until the custard sets.

8. Remove from oven and cool to room temperature, 20–30 minutes, then drizzle with honey, top with chopped pistachios or any fruit of your choice, and dust with the remaining 2 teaspoons of cinnamon or powdered sugar.

9. Serve warm and refrigerate leftovers in an airtight container for up to 3 days.

NUTRITION · PER ONE SERVING

Calories **629 (29%)**
Total Fat **44.46 g (92%)**
  Saturated Fat **24.554 g**
  Polyunsaturated Fat **3.101 g**
  Monounsaturated Fat **14.373 g**
  Trans Fat **0.01 g**
Cholesterol **206 mg**
Sodium **288 mg (19%)**
Total Carbohydrate: **48.29 g (20%)**
  Dietary Fiber: **1.6 g (6%)**
  Total Sugars: **22.95 g**

Protein: **9.72 g (18%)**
Vitamin A **1504 mcg (64%)**
Vitamin C **0.8 mcg (1%)**
Vitamin D **47 mcg (8%)**
Potassium **205 mg (4%)**
Calcium **82 mg (8%)**
Iron **2.46 mg (14%)**

MAIN DESSERTS

Pistachio Pudding

Makes 6 servings

PREP TIME: 30 minutes • **COOK TIME:** 13 minutes • **TOTAL TIME:** 4 hours 43 minutes
Level 3: Moderate

Once you make this pudding, you'll never go back to the boxed version. While pistachios are the star in this recipe, the orange zest brightens the flavor. The most difficult part of making this luscious pudding is deciding whether or not to share!

INGREDIENTS

1 cup shelled pistachios, raw and unsalted or 1 cup of pecans

½ cup granulated sugar, divided

2 cups + 2 tablespoons whole milk, divided

1 tablespoon orange zest

2 large egg yolks

1 large egg

2 tablespoons cornstarch

⅛ teaspoon sea salt

2 tablespoons unsalted butter

1 tablespoon vanilla extract

INSTRUCTIONS

1. Add the pistachios to a food processor bowl and finely chop.

2. Add ¼ cup of the sugar and 2 tablespoons of the milk to the nuts and continue processing, until a paste forms.

3. Whisk together the pistachio paste, remaining milk, and orange zest in a saucepan set over medium-high heat, until smooth. Cook for 4–5 minutes, whisking constantly to remove any lumps that may form. Once the mixture comes to a simmer and starts to steam, remove from heat.

4. In a small bowl, whisk together the remaining sugar, eggs, cornstarch, and salt until smooth and pale yellow.

5. Whisk ½ cup of the hot milk mixture into the egg mixture to temper them so they do not curdle. Gradually add the egg mixture to hot milk mixture in the saucepan, while whisking constantly. Cook for an additional 5–8 minutes over medium-low heat, until the custard thickens. Remove from heat.

6. Add the butter and vanilla extract, stirring just until the butter melts.

7. Pour into 6 dessert glasses and cover with plastic wrap pressed directly onto the surface of the pudding to keep a film from forming.

8. Refrigerate for 4–6 hours.

9. Serve cold and top with a dollop of whipped cream, chopped pistachios or pecans, if desired. Refrigerate leftovers in an airtight container for up to 3 days.

NUTRITION · PER ONE SERVING

Calories **325 (15%)**
Total Fat **16.56 g (34%)**
  Saturated Fat **4.958 g**
  Polyunsaturated Fat **3.4 g**
  Monounsaturated Fat **7.189 g**
  Trans Fat **0.003 g**
Cholesterol **105 mg**
Sodium **106 mg (7%)**
Total Carbohydrate: **36.41 g (15%)**
  Dietary Fiber: **2.2 g (9%)**
  Total Sugars: **29 g**

Protein: **8.83 g (16%)**
Vitamin A **387 mcg (17%)**
Vitamin C **2 mcg (3%)**
Vitamin D **60 mcg (10%)**
Potassium **335 mg (7%)**
Calcium **125 mg (13%)**
Iron **1.26 mg (7%)**

MAIN DESSERTS

Fig Walnut Cookies

Makes 20 servings

PREP TIME: 25 minutes • **COOK TIME:** 20 minutes • **TOTAL TIME:** 45 minutes

Level 3: Moderate

Nothing satisfies a craving better than a sweet dessert that's high in fiber and these cookies are the perfect example! A unique cross between bread and a cookie, this tasty, chewy treat will get you experimenting with a versatile and classic Mediterranean ingredient—figs.

INGREDIENTS

- ½ cup granulated sugar
- ½ cup brown sugar
- ½ cup unsalted butter, softened
- 1 large egg
- 1 teaspoon vanilla extract
- 2 cups all-purpose flour
- 1 teaspoon baking soda
- 1 teaspoon baking powder
- 1 teaspoon ground cinnamon
- ½ teaspoon nutmeg
- ½ teaspoon sea salt
- 1 cup figs, peeled and chopped
- ½ cup walnuts, chopped

INSTRUCTIONS

1. Preheat oven to 350°F and line 2 cookie sheets with parchment paper.

2. Combine both sugars with the unsalted butter in the bowl of a stand mixer outfitted with the paddle attachment. Beat for 1 minute, until smooth. Add the egg and vanilla extract and continue beating until light and fluffy.

3. Whisk together the all-purpose flour, baking soda, baking powder, cinnamon, nutmeg, and salt in a separate medium bowl.

4. With the mixer on low, gradually add the spiced flour mixture and beat just until combined. Fold in the figs and walnuts.

5. Scoop rounded tablespoons of the batter onto the prepared cookie sheets, leaving 2-inch spaces between them. Bake the cookies for 15–20 minutes, until brown around the edges.

6. Cool cookies on the pan for 5 minutes, then transfer to a wire rack to cool completely. Serve and enjoy! Refrigerate leftovers in an airtight container for up to 3 days.

NUTRITION · PER ONE SERVING

- Calories **139 (6%)**
- Total Fat **5.37 g (11%)**
  - Saturated Fat **2.218 g**
  - Polyunsaturated Fat **1.589 g**
  - Monounsaturated Fat **1.268 g**
  - *Trans* Fat **0 g**
- Cholesterol **15 mg**
- Sodium **126 mg (8%)**
- Total Carbohydrate: **21.12 g (9%)**
  - Dietary Fiber: **0.7 g (3%)**
  - Total Sugars: **10.88 g**
- Protein: **2.09 g (4%)**
- Vitamin A **112 mcg (5%)**
- Vitamin C **0.1 mcg**
- Vitamin D **4 mcg (1%)**
- Potassium **71 mg (2%)**
- Calcium **26 mg (3%)**
- Iron **0.83 mg (5%)**

Apricot Clafoutis

Makes 8 servings

PREP TIME: 30 minutes • **COOK TIME:** 45 minutes • **TOTAL TIME:** 1 hour 15 minutes
Level 3: Moderate

Don't be intimidated by the French pedigree of Clafoutis because it's surprisingly easy to make. Essentially, all you have to do is pour the crêpe-like batter over fresh apricots and bake it until the custard sets. Dust it with powdered sugar and—if you're feeling a bit extravagant or want to impress guests—serve with whipped cream!

INGREDIENTS

2 tablespoons unsalted butter, softened

6 apricots, pitted and quartered

1⅓ cups whole milk

3 large eggs, room temperature

¾ cup granulated sugar, divided

½ cup all-purpose flour

1 teaspoon ground cinnamon

1 teaspoon vanilla extract

½ teaspoon almond extract

INSTRUCTIONS

1. Preheat oven to 375°F and brush a 9-inch shallow pie plate with the softened butter.

2. Arrange the apricots in a single layer in the pie plate.

3. Whisk together the milk, eggs, ½ cup of the sugar, flour, cinnamon, vanilla extract, and almond extract in a medium bowl until smooth.

4. Pour the batter over the apricots and sprinkle the remaining ¼ cup of sugar on top.

5. Bake the Apricot Clafoutis for 45 minutes, until the custard is set.

6. Remove from oven and allow to cool in the pie plate for 15 minutes. Serve warm or at room temperature. Refrigerate leftovers in an airtight container for up to 3 days.

NUTRITION · PER ONE SERVING

Calories **191 (9%)**
Total Fat **5.09 g (10%)**
   Saturated Fat **2.544 g**
   Polyunsaturated Fat **0.476 g**
   Monounsaturated Fat **1.691 g**
   Trans Fat **0 g**
Cholesterol **77 mg**
Sodium **23 mg (2%)**
Total Carbohydrate: **33.44 g (14%)**
   Dietary Fiber: **0.9 g (4%)**
   Total Sugars: **26.48 g**

Protein: **3.54 g (6%)**
Vitamin A **720 mcg (31%)**
Vitamin C **2.6 mcg (3%)**
Vitamin D **35 mcg (6%)**
Potassium **140 mg (3%)**
Calcium **61 mg (6%)**
Iron **0.74 mg (4%)**

Spiced Walnut Fruitcake

Makes 7 servings

PREP TIME: 30 minutes • **COOK TIME:** 55 minutes • **TOTAL TIME:** 1 hour 35 minutes
Level 3: Moderate

One bite of this and you will understand why fruitcakes have been popular since Roman times! This version is studded with Mediterranean favorites, including walnuts, coconut, and dates. The variety of fragrant spices enhance flavor and transform this dessert from a typical fruitcake to an extraordinary one—to be enjoyed year-round.

INGREDIENTS

- 1 cup brown rice flour
- 1 cup almond flour
- ½ cup monk fruit sweetener
- 2 teaspoons baking powder
- 1 teaspoon ground cinnamon
- ½ teaspoon ground nutmeg
- ½ teaspoon ground ginger
- ½ teaspoon ground cloves
- ½ teaspoon ground cardamom
- ¼ teaspoon sea salt
- ⅓ cup extra-virgin olive oil
- 2 large eggs
- ⅓ cup almond milk
- 1 teaspoon vanilla extract
- 1 teaspoon almond extract
- 1 cup walnuts, chopped and roasted
- ½ cup unsweetened coconut flakes
- ½ cup dates, pitted and chopped

INSTRUCTIONS

1. Preheat oven to 350°F and coat a round 7-inch or a 8 × 4 × 2 ½ inch loaf pan with non-stick cooking spray.

2. Whisk together the flours, monk fruit sweetener, baking powder, cinnamon, nutmeg, ginger, cloves, cardamom, and salt in a large bowl.

3. Whisk together the olive oil, eggs, almond milk, vanilla extract, and almond extract in a separate small bowl, until well combined.

4. Add the olive oil mixture to the dry Ingredients, stirring just until incorporated. Fold in the walnuts, coconut flakes, and dates.

5. Pour the batter into the prepared cake pan and bake for 35–55 minutes, until a skewer comes out clean.

6. Cool for 10 minutes in the pan then remove to a wire rack to cool completely. Serve and enjoy! Refrigerate leftovers in an airtight container for up to 3 days.

NUTRITION · PER ONE SERVING

- Calories **359 (16%)**
- Total Fat **22.18 g (46%)**
  - Saturated Fat **4.719 g**
  - Polyunsaturated Fat **7.037 g**
  - Monounsaturated Fat **9.515 g**
  - *Trans* Fat **0.011 g**
- Cholesterol **55 mg**
- Sodium **140 mg (9%)**
- Total Carbohydrate: **35.29 g (14%)**
  - Dietary Fiber: **3.6 g (14%)**
  - Total Sugars: **10.69 g**
- Protein: **6.93 g (13%)**
- Vitamin A **178 mcg (8%)**
- Vitamin C **0.4 mcg (1%)**
- Vitamin D **12 mcg (2%)**
- Potassium **430 mg (9%)**
- Calcium **134 mg (13%)**
- Iron **1.53 mg (9%)**

MAIN DESSERTS

Italian Lemon Ricotta Cookies

Makes 25 servings

PREP TIME: 35 minutes • **COOK TIME:** 15 minutes • **TOTAL TIME:** 50 minutes
Level 3: Moderate

The Italians call these classic delicate cookies Biscotti Morbidi Ricotta e Limone. They are as perfect a dessert as they are paired with a morning cup of tea. The lemon and ricotta work together, creating an amazing fragrance and chewy texture. If you prefer your cookies extra crumbly, simply strain the ricotta cheese of any extra liquid.

INGREDIENTS

- 1¾ cups all-purpose flour
- 1 teaspoon ground cinnamon
- 1 teaspoon baking powder
- 1 teaspoon baking soda
- 1 cup ricotta cheese
- ¾ cup granulated sugar
- Zest of 1 lemon
- 1 large egg
- 2 tablespoons lemon juice
- 3 tablespoons powdered sugar

INSTRUCTIONS

1. Preheat oven to 350°F and line a cookie sheet with parchment paper.

2. Whisk together the flour, cinnamon, baking powder, and baking soda in a medium bowl.

3. Combine the ricotta, sugar, and lemon zest in the bowl of a stand mixer outfitted with the paddle attachment and beat until smooth. Add the egg and lemon juice and continue beating until combined.

4. Add the flour mixture and beat slowly just until the cookie dough comes together.

5. Shape batter into 25 walnut-sized balls leaving 2-inch spaces between them on the prepared cookie sheet.

6. Bake for 5–15 minutes or until brown around the edges.

7. Cool cookies on the pan for 5 minutes then transfer to a wire rack to cool completely.

8. Sift the powdered sugar onto the cookies and serve! Refrigerate leftovers in an airtight container for up to 3 days.

NUTRITION · PER ONE SERVING

Calories **250 (11%)**
Total Fat **4.91 g (10%)**
  Saturated Fat **2.814 g**
  Polyunsaturated Fat **0.354 g**
  Monounsaturated Fat **1.378 g**
  Trans Fat **0.002 g**
Cholesterol **39 mg**
Sodium **239 mg (16%)**
Total Carbohydrate: **44.68 g (18%)**
  Dietary Fiber: **0.9 g (4%)**
  Total Sugars: **22.08 g**

Protein: **7.15 g (13%)**
Vitamin A **173 mcg (7%)**
Vitamin C **3.8 mcg (5%)**
Vitamin D **8 mcg (1%)**
Potassium **82 mg (2%)**
Calcium **118 mg (12%)**
Iron **1.61 mg (9%)**

Middle Eastern Halva Shortbread

Makes 16 servings

PREP TIME: 45 minutes • **COOK TIME:** 42 minutes • **TOTAL TIME:** 5 hours 27 minutes
Level 4: Challenging

Halva is often described as a sweet Middle Eastern candy-like confection. While the Ingredients vary between regions, the popular treat can be eaten alone or baked into pastry desserts. This version mixes halva with cashew butter and coconut as a filling for a buttery, flaky shortbread, topped with luscious caramel.

INGREDIENTS

For the shortbread:

¾ cup unsalted butter, melted

¼ cup granulated sugar

¼ cup powdered sugar, sifted

3½ tablespoons cornstarch

½ teaspoon vanilla extract

2 cups all-purpose flour

½ teaspoon ground cardamom

¼ teaspoon salt

For the filling:

¾ cup halva, crumbled

⅓ cup cashew butter

¼ cup unsweetened coconut, shredded

For the topping:

1 cup granulated sugar

½ cup water

½ cup unsalted butter, cubed

⅓ cup heavy cream, room temperature

⅓ cup cashew butter

INSTRUCTIONS

1. Preheat oven to 400°F and line an 8-×-8-inch baking dish with parchment paper, making sure that parchment hangs over the sides to aid in removing the shortbread.

To make the shortbread:

1. Combine the butter, granulated sugar, powdered sugar, cornstarch, and vanilla extract in the bowl of a stand mixer outfitted with the paddle attachment and beat until combined.

2. Whisk together the flour, cardamom, and salt in a separate medium bowl.

3. Add to flour mixture to the stand mixer's bowl and beat slowly, until just combined.

4. Press the dough into the prepared pan in an even layer and bake for 25 minutes, or until golden brown. Allow to cool completely in the pan.

To make the filling:

1. Combine the halva, cashew butter, and shredded coconut in a small bowl, mixing well.

2. Spread the halva filling in an even layer over the cooled shortbread crust.

To make the caramel topping:

1. Combine the sugar and water in a saucepan set over medium-low heat, stirring occasionally for 4–5 minutes, until the sugar dissolves.

2. Increase heat to medium-high and continue cooking until the caramel forms and is a rich golden color, about 12 minutes.

3. Remove from heat and whisk in the butter and heavy cream, until well combined and the butter is melted. Whisk in the cashew butter.

recipe continues

4. Pour caramel over the halva filling, making sure to cover it completely.

5. Refrigerate for 4–6 hours, until set.

6. Cut into 16 squares and serve. Refrigerate leftovers in an airtight container for up to 3 days.

NUTRITION · PER ONE SERVING

Calories 299 (15%)	Protein: 2.36 g (4%)
Total Fat 20.33 g (40%)	Vitamin A 572 mcg (24%)
Saturated Fat 11.912 g	Vitamin C 0.7 mcg
Polyunsaturated Fat 0.749 g	Vitamin D 14 mcg (2%)
Monounsaturated Fat 5.046 g	Potassium 44 mg (1%)
Trans Fat 0.307 g (2%)	Calcium 17 mg (2%)
Cholesterol 42 mg	Iron 0.95 mg (5%)
Sodium 114 mg (7%)	
Total Carbohydrate: 23.15 g (9%)	
Dietary Fiber: 0.5 g (2%)	
Total Sugars: 12.4 g (3%)	

Date Almond Brownies

Makes 16 servings

PREP TIME: 40 minutes • **COOK TIME:** 30 minutes • **TOTAL TIME:** 1 hour 10 minutes
Level 3: Moderate

You can always count on the caramel-like flavor of Medjool dates to add the perfect amount of sweetness to any recipe. Brimming with fiber and antioxidants, these brownies can improve digestion. The toasted almonds and shredded coconut paired with a touch of espresso powder, make this dessert the definition of velvety goodness!

INGREDIENTS

½ cup unsweetened coconut, shredded

½ cup almonds

1 cup Medjool dates, pitted

¾ cup hot water

¾ cup almond flour

½ cup unsweetened cocoa powder

3 tablespoons stevia

1 tablespoon vanilla extract

1 teaspoon espresso powder

1 teaspoon baking powder

¼ teaspoon sea salt

INSTRUCTIONS

1. Preheat oven to 350°F and line a cookie sheet with parchment paper. Coat an 8-×-8-inch baking dish with non-stick cooking spray.

2. Evenly spread the shredded coconut and almonds in a single layer onto the prepared cookie sheet and bake 8–10 minutes, stirring every two minutes, until coconut is golden. Set aside to cool completely.

3. Combine the dates and hot water in a small bowl for 10 minutes, allowing the dates to soften.

4. Drain the dates and transfer to a food processor, blending into a smooth paste.

5. Add the almond flour, cocoa powder, stevia, vanilla extract, espresso powder, baking powder, and salt to the food processor's bowl and blend well, scraping down the sides as needed, until a smooth batter is formed.

6. Remove lid and blade from the food processor and fold in the toasted almonds and coconut.

recipe continues

7. Pour batter into the prepared baking dish and bake for 18–20 minutes or until the center of the cake springs back when lightly touched.

8. Cool for 10 minutes in the pan, then transfer to a wire rack, cooling completely.

9. Cut into 16 squares and serve. Refrigerate leftovers in an airtight container for up to 3 days.

NUTRITION · PER ONE SERVING

Calories **101 (5%)**
Total Fat **4.85 g (10%)**
  Saturated Fat **0.561 g**
  Polyunsaturated Fat **1.112 g**
  Monounsaturated Fat **2.935 g**
  Trans Fat **0.001 g**
Cholesterol **0 mg**
Sodium **68 mg (5%)**
Total Carbohydrate: **19.89 g (8%)**
  Dietary Fiber: **2.9 g (12%)**
  Total Sugars: **10.16 g**

Protein: **2.69 g (5%)**
Vitamin A **21 mcg (1%)**
Vitamin C **0.2 mcg**
Vitamin D **0 mcg**
Potassium **252 mg (5%)**
Calcium **60 mg (6%)**
Iron **0.93 mg (5%)**

Lebanese Semolina Pudding

Makes 6–8 servings

PREP TIME: 20 minutes • **COOK TIME:** 5 minutes • **TOTAL TIME:** 4 hours 25 minutes
Level 3: Moderate

Layali Lubnan, as it's called in Lebanese, is a traditional treat that is so easy to make it ranks as one of the most-served desserts! There are many variations, and true to tradition, mine incorporates pistachios and orange flavoring, but uniquely adds rose water. If you're in the mood to try something new, this vegan-friendly dish fits the bill.

INGREDIENTS

For the pudding:

3½ cups almond milk

¾ cup fine semolina

½ cup granulated sugar

¼ teaspoon sea salt

½ cup dried currants, chopped

2 teaspoons rose water

1½ teaspoons orange extract

½ teaspoon vanilla extract

¾ cup pistachios, chopped

For the whipped cream:

¾ cup coconut cream, chilled*

3 tablespoons powdered sugar

INSTRUCTIONS

To make the pudding:

1. Whisk together the almond milk, semolina, sugar, and salt in a large saucepan set over medium-high heat. Whisk constantly for 4–5 minutes, until it boils and continue boiling for 30 seconds.

2. Remove pan from heat and stir in the dried currants, rose water, orange extract, and vanilla extract.

3. Pour the hot pudding into 6 or 8 dessert dishes, smooth the top of each pudding, and allow to cool completely at room temperature.

4. Once cooled, cover each dish with plastic wrap and press it directly against the surface of the pudding. Chill in the fridge for 4–6 hours.

To make the whipped cream:

1. Pour the coconut cream into the chilled bowl** of a stand mixer outfitted with the whisk attachment and whip for 30 seconds.

2. Add the powdered sugar and whip for another 30 seconds, until a fluffy whipped cream forms.

3. Top each pudding with a dollop of whipped cream or any fruit of your choice before serving. Refrigerate leftovers in an airtight container for up to 3 days.

NOTES: *Chill 1½ cups of coconut cream in the refrigerator overnight. The cream will separate, forming a solid layer on top. When ready, scoop out the thickened top layer until you have ¾ cup.

**Place mixer bowl in the freezer for 10–15 minutes before adding the coconut cream.

NUTRITION • PER ONE SERVING

Calories **326 (15%)**
Total Fat **16.71 g (34%)**
  Saturated Fat **9.576 g**
  Polyunsaturated Fat **1.953 g**
  Monounsaturated Fat **3.969 g**
  Trans Fat **0 g**
Cholesterol **11 mg**
Sodium **120 mg (8%)**
Total Carbohydrate: **37.78 g (15%)**
  Dietary Fiber: **2.6 g (10%)**
  Total Sugars: **22.31 g**

Protein: **8.61 g (16%)**
Vitamin A **224 mcg (10%)**
Vitamin C **4.5 mcg (6%)**
Vitamin D **2 mcg**
Potassium **383 mg (8%)**
Calcium **141 mg (14%)**
Iron **1.27 mg (7%)**

Olive Oil Chocolate Chip Cookies

Makes 24 cookies

PREP TIME: 35 minutes • **COOK TIME:** 12 minutes • **TOTAL TIME:** 47 minutes
Level 3: Moderate

Like most of us, you've probably baked more than your fair share of chocolate chip cookies and aren't keen to try another recipe. Before you pass this one by, I'm pretty sure it may well become your favorite. Substituting olive oil for butter gives these cookies a healthier edge, plus they are as perfect for dessert as they are for an afternoon pick-me-up.

INGREDIENTS

2 cups all-purpose flour

1 teaspoon sea salt

½ teaspoon baking soda

1 cup extra-virgin olive oil

1 cup light brown sugar

½ cup granulated sugar

1 tablespoon vanilla extract

1 large egg

2 cups semisweet chocolate chips

INSTRUCTIONS

1. Preheat oven to 350°F and line 2 cookie sheets with parchment paper.

2. Whisk together flour, salt, and baking soda in a small bowl and set aside.

3. Whisk together the olive oil, brown sugar, granulated sugar, and vanilla extract in a separate large bowl. Add the egg and whisk until smooth.

4. Add the wet Ingredients to the dry Ingredients in batches, stirring until well incorporated. Fold in the chocolate chips.

5. Roll the cookie dough into 24 balls (about 2 tablespoons each) and place on the prepared cookie sheets leaving 2-inch spaces between them. Slightly flatten each ball with the palm of your hand.

6. Bake both cookie sheets at the same time for 10–12 minutes, until the edges are golden brown.

7. Cool cookies on the pan for 5 minutes, then remove to a wire rack to cool completely. Serve and enjoy! Refrigerate leftovers in an airtight container for up to 3 days.

NUTRITION · PER ONE SERVING

Calories **226 (10%)**
Total Fat **9.11 g (19%)**
   Saturated Fat **3.552 g**
   Polyunsaturated Fat **0.47 g**
   Monounsaturated Fat **2.941 g**
   Trans Fat **0.009 g**
Cholesterol **12 mg**
Sodium **207 mg (14%)**
Total Carbohydrate: **33.66 g (14%)**
   Dietary Fiber: **1.5 g (6%)**
   Total Sugars: **23.19 g**

Protein: **2.22 g (4%)**
Vitamin A **32 mcg (1%)**
Vitamin C **0 mcg**
Vitamin D **2 mcg**
Potassium **30 mg (1%)**
Calcium **17 mg (2%)**
Iron **1.14 mg (6%)**

Pear Frangipane Tart

Makes 8 servings

PREP TIME: 1 hour 5 minutes • **COOK TIME:** 1 hour 35 minutes • **TOTAL TIME:** 4 hours 10 minutes

Level 5: Ambitious

The dough of this traditional French tart is loaded with almond cream called frangipane. Don't be put off by the length of this recipe, because making it is totally worth the effort! The key ingredient is the pears—slightly ripe Comice pears are perfect as they are extremely juicy with a buttery sweet taste.

INGREDIENTS

For the dough:

2 cups unbleached all-purpose flour

⅓ cup granulated sugar

1 teaspoon orange zest

¼ teaspoon sea salt

⅓ cup unsalted butter, chilled and cubed

1 large egg yolk

1 teaspoon vanilla extract

For the poached pears:

6 cups cold water

2 cups granulated sugar

2 2-inch cinnamon sticks

2 tablespoons orange zest

2 tablespoons lemon juice

1 tablespoon star anise

1 teaspoon cardamom

1 teaspoon cloves

1 tablespoon vanilla extract

3 large pears, slightly ripe

1 lemon wedge

For the frangipane:

½ cup unsalted butter, softened

½ cup granulated sugar

1 cup almond flour

3 large eggs, room temperature

INSTRUCTIONS

To make the dough:

1. Coat a 10-inch shallow pie pan with a removable bottom with non-stick cooking spray.

2. Combine the flour, sugar, orange zest, and salt in the bowl of a food processor and pulse until combined.

3. Add the cubed butter and pulse until the mixture resembles fine crumbs.

4. Add the egg yolk and vanilla extract and process until the dough begins holding together.

5. Remove the dough to a clean, floured surface, and knead until smooth. Press into the bottom and sides of the prepared pan. Chill dough in the fridge for 1 hour or in the freezer for 30 minutes.

To make the poached pears:

1. Combine the water and sugar in a large pot set over medium-high heat, stirring periodically until it simmers and the sugar dissolves.

2. Stir in the cinnamon sticks, orange zest, lemon juice, star anise, cardamom, cloves, and vanilla extract. Turn off the heat.

3. Peel the pears, leaving the stem in place. Rub pears with the lemon wedge to prevent browning. Core and seed each pear, do this from the blossom end, with a small melon baller.

4. Return pot to a simmer and gently lower each pear into the poaching liquid using a large spoon.

5. Adjust heat to a low and simmer. Cover the pot with a round sheet of parchment paper. Simmer the pears, turning them periodically for 12–15 minutes, or until they are tender.

recipe and ingredients continue

1 tablespoon unbleached all-purpose flour

1 tablespoon dark rum

1 teaspoon vanilla extract

½ teaspoon lemon extract

2 tablespoons powdered sugar

6. Remove pot from heat. Cool pears completely in the poaching liquid.

7. Position oven rack in the center of the oven and preheat to 375°F.

8. Coat a piece of aluminum foil with butter and place butter-side down over the dough and cover the foil with dried beans or baking weights to keep it in place.

9. Place the pie pan on a cookie sheet and bake for 20 minutes.

10. Remove the aluminum foil and weights and continue baking for 10–15 minutes, until slightly golden.

11. Cool tart shell completely in the pan on a wire rack.

To make the frangipane:

1. Combine butter and sugar in the bowl of a stand mixer outfitted with the paddle attachment. Mix on low speed until creamy, and then gradually alternate adding the almond flour and the egg, mixing to incorporate after each addition.

2. Add the all-purpose flour and continue mixing on low, until combined.

3. Add the rum, vanilla extract, and lemon extract, mixing until combined.

4. Preheat oven to 375°F, place the pan with the cooked tart shell onto a cookie sheet, fill with the frangipane cream, and smooth the top.

5. Remove the cool pears from the poaching liquid and place onto paper towels to drain.

6. Cut each pear in half, remove the stem, and cut each half horizontally into thin slices, about ⅛-inch thick.

7. Carefully arrange the pear slices with a spatula to resemble petals of a flower on the frangipane filling, with the narrow end of each slice facing the center.

8. Bake for 40–55 minutes, until golden brown.

9. Allow to cool completely in the pan for 1–2 hours.

10. Dust with powdered sugar and unmold before serving. Refrigerate leftovers in an airtight container for up to 3 days.

NUTRITION · PER ONE SERVING

Calories **602 (28%)**
Total Fat **27.26 g (19%)**
  Saturated Fat **12.745 g**
  Polyunsaturated Fat **2.847 g**
  Monounsaturated Fat **10.169 g**
  Trans Fat **0.01 g**
Cholesterol **128 mg**
Sodium **120 mg (8%)**
Total Carbohydrate: **80.56 g (33%)**
  Dietary Fiber: **5.8 g (23%)**
Total Sugars: **46.32 g**

Protein: **10.22 g (19%)**
Vitamin A **730 mcg (31%)**
Vitamin C **10.1 mcg (13%)**
Vitamin D **33 mcg (6%)**
Potassium **313 mg (7%)**
Calcium **110 mg (11%)**
Iron **3.32 mg (18%)**

Roasted Fig & Apricot Gelato

Makes 10 servings

PREP TIME: 35 minutes • **COOK TIME:** 15 minutes
TOTAL TIME: 4 hours 50 minutes + overnight

Level 5: Ambitious

This Roasted Fig & Apricot Gelato is the creamiest you'll ever taste! The mascarpone cheese is responsible for its scoopable texture, even when frozen. If you're hoping to serve a real showstopper, look no further.

INGREDIENTS

- 1½ cups fresh figs, halved
- 4 apricots, pitted and halved
- ¼ cup brown sugar
- 2 cups heavy cream
- 14 ounces sweetened condensed milk
- 8 ounces mascarpone cheese
- ½ cup granulated sugar
- 1 teaspoon ground cinnamon
- 1 teaspoon vanilla extract
- 1 tablespoon balsamic vinegar
- 1 tablespoon whisky
- 1 tablespoon lemon zest
- Juice of 1 lemon

INSTRUCTIONS

1. Place the base of the ice-cream maker in the freezer at a least one day before.

2. Preheat oven to 400°F and line a cookie sheet with parchment paper.

3. Arrange the figs and apricots flesh side up on the prepared cookie sheet and sprinkle with brown sugar. Roast for 15 minutes, or until fruit is soft.

4. Cool fruit slightly before placing in the bowl of a food processor and blending into a smooth purée, scraping down the sides of the bowl, as needed.

5. Pour the purée into a container, cover, and chill overnight.

6. Combine the heavy cream, condensed milk, mascarpone cheese, sugar, cinnamon, and vanilla extract in a blender and process until smooth.

7. Pour into a bowl and cover with plastic wrap pressed directly onto the surface of the cream mixture, chill overnight.

8. Combine the fruit purée and the cream and churn in an ice cream machine following the manufacturer's Instructions.

9. Five minutes before the end of the churning time add the balsamic vinegar, whisky, lemon zest, and lemon juice. Continue processing for the remaining time.

10. Transfer the gelato to an airtight container and freeze for 3–4 hours, or until it sets.

11. Serve and enjoy! Refrigerate leftovers in an airtight container for up to 3 days.

NUTRITION · PER ONE SERVING

Calories **462 (21%)**
Total Fat **29.06 g (60%)**
  Saturated Fat **17.554 g**
  Polyunsaturated Fat **1.2 g**
  Monounsaturated Fat **8.63 g**
  Trans Fat **0.84g**
Cholesterol **104 mg**
Sodium **154 mg (10%)**
Total Carbohydrate: **46.57 g (19%)**
  Dietary Fiber: **1.9 g (8%)**
  Total Sugars: **43.95 g**

Protein: **6.09 g (11%)**
Vitamin A **1454 mcg (62%)**
Vitamin C **6.2 mcg (8%)**
Vitamin D **21 mcg (4%)**
Potassium **387 mg (8%)**
Calcium **194 mg (19%)**
Iron **0.5 mg (3%)**

Greek Pumpkin Pie (Kolokythópita)

Makes 30 servings

PREP TIME: 40 minutes • **COOK TIME:** 30 minutes • **TOTAL TIME:** 1 hour 10 minutes
Level 3: Moderate

This recipe follows the traditional method of many Greek grandmothers, but without the added stress of making phyllo from scratch! Instead of pouring pumpkin filling into a pie shell, these flaky phyllo-filled logs are stuffed with a creamy sweet pumpkin filling and dusted with powdered sugar. Swap out your traditional pumpkin pie for this version and your next holiday dinner will have you blushing from all the compliments.

INGREDIENTS

2 cups pumpkin purée

½ cup granulated sugar

½ cup pecans, finely ground

⅓ cup brown sugar

¼ cup unsalted butter, melted and divided

2 teaspoons pumpkin pie spice

12 phyllo sheets, thawed

1 tablespoon extra-virgin olive oil

4 tablespoons powdered sugar

INSTRUCTIONS

1. Preheat oven to 350°F and line a cookie sheet with parchment paper.

2. Combine the pumpkin purée, granulated sugar, pecans, brown sugar, 2 teaspoons of butter, and pumpkin pie spice in a medium bowl, mixing well.

3. Place a sheet of phyllo on a large flat surface, like a table or kitchen counter, and brush it with olive oil, then top with a second sheet of phyllo and brush it with butter.

4. Spread ¼ cup of the pumpkin mixture along the short edge of the phyllo and gently roll to encase the filling in a log shape.

5. Brush both the top and bottom of the log with olive oil, then place seam-side down on the prepared cookie sheet. With a sharp knife, cut 4 slits spaced 2½-inches apart, across the top of each log.

recipe continues

6. Repeat steps 4–5 until you have 6 logs.

7. Bake for 30 minutes, until golden. Cool in the pan for 10 minutes, then transfer to a serving plate.

8. Dust with powdered sugar before serving. Refrigerate leftovers in an airtight container for up to 3 days.

NUTRITION · PER ONE SERVING

Calories **76 (3%)**
Total Fat **2.73 g (6%)**
  Saturated Fat **0.886 g**
  Polyunsaturated Fat **0.468 g**
  Monounsaturated Fat **1.217 g**
  Trans Fat **0 g**
Cholesterol **2 mg**
Sodium **39 mg (3%)**
Total Carbohydrate: **12.4 g (5%)**
  Dietary Fiber: **0.8 g (3%)**
  Total Sugars: **7.34 g**

Protein: **0.94 g (2%)**
Vitamin A **2575 mcg (110%)**
Vitamin C **0.7 mcg (1%)**
Vitamin D **1**
Potassium **51 mg (1%)**
Calcium **10 mg (1%)**
Iron **0.57 mg (3%)**

Saffron-Infused Vanilla Bavarois

Makes 6 servings

PREP TIME: 40 minutes • **COOK TIME:** 20 minutes • **TOTAL TIME:** 1 hour + overnight
Level 5: Ambitious

Served with a lovely spiced saffron-infused syrup, this Vanilla Bavarois is simply divine. With protein-rich yogurt as its secret ingredient, this healthy treat will keep you fueled and satisfied for hours. Not only does it make the perfect dessert, it also works as a nutritious breakfast or snack.

INGREDIENTS

For the bavarois:

4 sheets gelatin

1 cup cold water

1 vanilla bean

1¼ cups heavy cream, divided

⅔ cup granulated sugar

2½ cups plain Greek yogurt

½ cup pistachios, coarsely chopped

For the spiced saffron-infused syrup:

⅓ cup maple syrup

1 2-inch cinnamon stick

2 tablespoons water

1 tablespoon saffron threads

1 teaspoon ground cardamom

INSTRUCTIONS

To make the bavarois:

1. Combine the gelatin sheets and cold water in a small bowl and set aside for 3–5 minutes, until the gelatin softens.

2. Slice the vanilla bean in half and remove the seeds, add both to a saucepan along with ¾ cup of the heavy cream and sugar. Bring to a boil over medium-high heat. Remove from heat.

3. Drain excess water before adding the gelatin to the pot of hot cream and stir until dissolved.

4. Place yogurt in a large bowl and whisk until smooth.

5. Add the vanilla cream mixture and continue whisking until smooth and well combined. Remove the vanilla bean seeds and continue whisking until mixture cools and thickens.

6. Add the remaining ½ cup of heavy cream to the bowl of a stand mixer outfitted with the whisk attachment and whip until soft peaks form.

recipe continues

7. Fold the whipped heavy cream into cooled cream mixture and then ladle equal portions into 6 (6-oz.) molds and refrigerate overnight.

To make the spiced saffron-infused syrup:

1. Combine the maple syrup, cinnamon stick, water, saffron, and ground cinnamon in a small saucepan, and bring to a simmer over medium-high heat. Remove from heat and cool slightly.

2. Dip the bavarois molds in hot water and invert on individual serving dishes to unstick.

3. Drizzle each with the saffron-infused syrup and a sprinkle of chopped pistachios before serving. Refrigerate leftovers in an airtight container for up to 3 days.

NUTRITION · PER ONE SERVING

Calories **314 (14%)**
Total Fat **17.29 g (36%)**
  Saturated Fat **8.482 g**
  Polyunsaturated Fat **1.861 g**
  Monounsaturated Fat **6.035 g**
  Trans Fat **0 g**
Cholesterol **48 mg**
Sodium **70 mg (5%)**
Total Carbohydrate: **31.89 g (13%)**
  Dietary Fiber: **1.4 g (6%)**
  Total Sugars: **27.66 g**

Protein: **10.24 g (19%)**
Vitamin A **518 mcg (22%)**
Vitamin C **1.6 mcg (2%)**
Vitamin D **9 mcg (2%)**
Potassium **332 mg (7%)**
Calcium **182 mg (18%)**
Iron **0.67 mg (4%)**

Classic Profiteroles

Makes 48 servings

PREP TIME: 1 hour 10 minutes • **COOK TIME:** 36 minutes • **TOTAL TIME:** 1 hour 46 minutes
Level 5: Ambitious

Whether you call it a cream puff, profiterole, or chou à la crème, this elegant French pastry has been a favorite since it's American debut in 1851. Pop one of these chocolate drizzled delights into your mouth to experience whipped cream oozing from the fluffy pastry and you'll see why it's still an international favorite!

INGREDIENTS

For the dough:

½ cup unsalted butter

1 cup water

1 cup all-purpose flour

¼ teaspoon sea salt

4 large eggs, room temperature

For the chocolate drizzle:

1 cup heavy cream

8 ounces semi-sweet dark chocolate

For the filling:

2 cups heavy cream

¼ cup powdered sugar

1 tablespoon vanilla extract

INSTRUCTIONS

To make the dough:

1. Place the butter in a small pot set over low heat until melted.

2. Add the water and raise the heat to medium-high. Bring to a simmer and remove from heat.

3. Add the flour and salt, stirring with a wooden spoon for about 1 minute, until the profiterole dough forms a ball and pulls away from the sides of the pot.

4. Cool dough in the pot for 10 minutes.

5. Preheat oven to 420°F and lightly coat two cookie sheets with non-stick spray.

6. Place cooled dough in a bowl and add the eggs one at a time, stirring well after each addition, until the dough resembles a thick paste.

7. Transfer the dough to a piping bag outfitted with a star tip and pipe small round mounds of dough (of approximately 2 teaspoons) onto the prepared cookie sheets leaving at least 2-inches of space between each one.

recipe continues

8. Bake for 7 minutes, then rotate pans and bake for an additional 9–12 minutes. Remove pan from oven and pierce the top of each profiterole with a knife to create a hole for the filling. Continue baking for an additional 5–7 minutes, until golden and crispy.

9. Transfer the profiteroles to a wire rack to cool completely.

To make the chocolate drizzle:

1. Combine the heavy cream and chocolate in a microwave-safe bowl. Set microwave power at 20% and heat at 30-second increments, stirring after each, until chocolate is melted and smooth. Allow the chocolate to cool slightly.

To make the filling:

1. Add the heavy cream to the bowl of a stand mixer outfitted with a whisk attachment and whip it for 1 minute. Add the powdered sugar and vanilla extract and whip for 5–8 minutes, until stiff peaks form.

2. Transfer the whipped cream to a piping bag outfitted with a small nozzle and squeeze it into the holes in the cooled profiteroles.

3. Drizzle the profiteroles with chocolate and let sit for 10–15 minutes, to set the chocolate before serving. Refrigerate leftovers in an airtight container for up to 3 days.

NUTRITION · PER ONE SERVING

Calories **105 (5%)**	Protein: **1.38 g (3%)**
Total Fat **8.62 g (18%)**	Vitamin A **227 mcg (12%)**
Saturated Fat **5.184 g**	Vitamin C **0.1 mcg**
Polyunsaturated Fat **0.386 g**	Vitamin D **8 mcg (1%)**
Monounsaturated Fat **2.566 g**	Potassium **42 mg (1%)**
Trans Fat **0.002 g**	Calcium **16 mg (2%)**
Cholesterol **38 mg**	Iron **0.48 mg (3%)**
Sodium **26 mg (2%)**	
Total Carbohydrate: **5.83 g (2%)**	
Dietary Fiber: **0.4 g (2%)**	
Total Sugars: **3.29 g**	

Pistachio Pavlova with Berries

Makes 6 servings

PREP TIME: 45 minutes • **COOK TIME:** 2 hours • **TOTAL TIME:** 2 hours 45 minutes
Level 5: Ambitious

A pavlova is a meringue-based dessert created in the 1920s and named in honour of a famous dancer of the era, Anna Pavlova. While still popular today, it's now known as "the pav," a term that literally translates to "meringue." This lovely Pistachio Pavlova with Berries is true to its heritage—crispy on the outside and soft, yet chewy on the inside, like a golden marshmallow.

INGREDIENTS

½ cup shelled unsalted pistachios, roasted and divided

4 large egg whites

1 cup granulated sugar

1 tablespoon cornstarch

1 teaspoon white vinegar

1 teaspoon vanilla extract

1 cup heavy cream

2 tablespoons powdered sugar

½ cup fresh strawberries, diced

½ cup fresh blueberries

½ cup fresh raspberries

½ cup fresh blackberries

INSTRUCTIONS

1. Preheat oven to 350°F and line a cookie sheet with parchment paper.

2. Process ¼ cup of the pistachios in a food processor by pulsing to form both coarse and fine pieces.

3. Sift pistachios pieces in a fine-mesh sieve over a bowl and shake gently to remove any nut "dust." Set pistachio pieces aside.

4. Add the egg whites to the bowl of a stand mixer bowl outfitted with the whisk attachment and whip until fluffy. Continue to whip while gradually adding the sugar, 1 tablespoon at a time, until egg whites are stiff and glossy.

5. Whisk together the sifted pistachios, cornstarch, vinegar, and vanilla extract in a separate medium bowl. Once combined, fold into the egg white mixture.

recipe continues

6. Spread the egg white mixture onto the prepared cookie sheet to form a 10-inch circle. Place pan in oven and immediate decrease temperature to 275°F. Bake for 1 hour. Then turn off heat and let meringue stay in oven for another hour.

7. Transfer meringue to a wire rack to cool completely.

8. Add the heavy cream to the bowl of a stand mixer outfitted with a whisk attachment and whip for 1 minute. Add the powdered sugar and beat for another 5–8 minutes, until stiff peaks form.

9. To serve, place the meringue onto a serving dish and spread the whipped cream over top. Add a mound of the mixed berries and finish with a sprinkle of the remaining ¼ cup of chopped pistachios. Refrigerate leftovers in an airtight container for up to 3 days.

NUTRITION · PER ONE SERVING

Calories **375 (17%)**
Total Fat **19.52 g (40%)**
  Saturated Fat **9.705 g**
  Polyunsaturated Fat **2.037 g**
  Monounsaturated Fat **6.69 g**
  Trans Fat **0 g**
Cholesterol **54 mg**
Sodium **55 mg (4%)**
Total Carbohydrate: **47.28 g (19%)**
  Dietary Fiber: **3 g (12%)**
  Total Sugars: **41.26 g**

Protein: **5.91 g (11%)**
Vitamin A **647 mcg (28%)**
Vitamin C **15.1 mcg (20%)**
Vitamin D **11 mcg (2%)**
Potassium **239 mg (5%)**
Calcium **48 mg (5%)**
Iron **0.73 mg (4%)**

Yogurt and Granola

Avocado Coconut Pudding

Makes 2 servings

PREP TIME: 15 minutes • **COOK TIME:** 0 • **TOTAL TIME:** 1 hour 15 minutes
Level 2: Easy

Coconut and avocado may seem like an odd duo, but these two superfoods combine surprisingly well to make a tasty and satisfying breakfast or lunch, as well as a dessert. Chock full of healthy fats and essential vitamins, this recipe may very well become your new favorite snack.

INGREDIENTS

½ cup chia seeds

⅓ cup + 2 tablespoons coconut milk, divided

2 teaspoons + 2 tablespoons maple syrup, divided

1 cup frozen or fresh raspberries

½ fresh banana

1 tablespoon ground turmeric

1 avocado, peeled, pitted, and sliced

½ cup granola

INSTRUCTIONS

1. Choose 2 (8-oz.) containers; these can be jars or bowls, glass, or plastic.*

2. Combine the chia seeds, 2 tablespoons of the coconut milk, and 2 teaspoons of the maple syrup in a small bowl, mixing well and set it aside.

3. Combine the remaining coconut milk and maple syrup, along with the raspberries, banana, turmeric, and avocado in a blender and process until smooth.

4. Divide the chia-seed coconut milk mixture evenly between your chosen containers, then top with mixture from the blender, creating two distinct layers. Sprinkle with granola.

5. Cover and chill for a minimum of 1 hour or overnight if you want to have this for breakfast.

NOTE: *Choose containers with well-fitting lids for an on-the-go breakfast, lunch, or snack.

NUTRITION · PER ONE SERVING

Calories **722 (33%)**
Total Fat **38.54 g (79%)**
  Saturated Fat **18.103 g**
  Polyunsaturated Fat **5.355 g**
  Monounsaturated Fat **12.361 g**
  Trans Fat **0.013 g**
Cholesterol **0 mg**
Sodium **119 mg (8%)**
Total Carbohydrate: **92.13 g (38%)**
  Dietary Fiber: **18.2 g (73%)**
  Total Sugars: **47.5 g**

Protein: **9.7 g (18%)**
Vitamin A **193 mcg (8%)**
Vitamin C **29 mcg (39%)**
Vitamin D **1 mcg**
Potassium **1110 mg (24%)**
Calcium **136 mg (14%)**
Iron **6.34 mg (35%)**

Blueberry Yogurt with Chickpea Topping

Makes 2 servings

PREP TIME: 15 minutes • **COOK TIME:** 12 minutes • **TOTAL TIME:** 4 hours 27 minutes
Level 2: Easy

Whoever said chickpeas should be reserved for dinner recipes hasn't tried this tempting dessert! If you've never caramelized chickpeas, brace yourself, as they make an excellent dessert topping. This light treat is a great ending to a heavy meal and is also perfect for breakfast.

INGREDIENTS

- 2 cups blueberries
- 3 tablespoons honey
- 1 teaspoon dried lavender
- Zest of 1 lemon
- Juice of 1 lemon
- 2 cups plain Greek yogurt
- 2 teaspoons unsalted butter
- ½ cup chickpeas, boiled and peeled
- 2 tablespoons granulated sugar

INSTRUCTIONS

1. Choose 2 (8-oz.) containers; these can be jars or bowls, glass, or plastic.*

2. Add the blueberries, honey, lavender, lemon zest, and lemon juice to a blender and process until well combined.

3. Pour into a medium bowl and add the yogurt, stirring briefly and only until streaks of the blueberry mixture are visible, giving a marbleized appearance. Set aside.

4. Melt the butter in a skillet set over medium-high heat.

5. Add the chickpeas and sugar and cook for 5 minutes, until the sugar melts and the chickpeas are caramelized.

6. Turn the chickpeas onto a silicone baking mat in a single layer and allow to cool completely.

7. Divide the caramelized chickpeas between 2 containers and top with the yogurt mixture. Top with your favorite fruit if desire.

recipe continues

8. Wrap with plastic wrap or place the lid on your containers and refrigerate for 3–4 hours. Serve and enjoy!

NOTE: *Choose containers with well-fitting lids for an on-the-go breakfast, lunch, or snack.

NUTRITION · PER ONE SERVING

Calories **492 (23%)**
Total Fat **13.49 g (25%)**
  Saturated Fat **7.738 g**
  Polyunsaturated Fat **1.068 g**
  Monounsaturated Fat **3.497 g**
  Trans Fat **0.156 g**
Cholesterol **42 mg**
Sodium **150 mg (10%)**
Total Carbohydrate: **84.96 g (38%)**
  Dietary Fiber: **7.1 g (28%)**
  Total Sugars: **67.47 g**

Protein: **13.49 g (25%)**
Vitamin A **455 mcg (20%)**
Vitamin C **29.4 mcg (39%)**
Vitamin D **8 mcg (1%)**
Potassium **663 mg (14%)**
Calcium **334 mg (33%)**
Iron **1.91 mg (11%)**

Graham Cracker Coriander Yogurt Cups

Makes 3 servings

PREP TIME: 20 minutes • **COOK TIME:** 0 • **TOTAL TIME:** 20 min + overnight
Level 2: Easy

Coriander has been used in Egyptian culture as medicine and in cooking since 1550 BC. This dessert features creamy yogurt and a cream cheese filling with a Graham cracker and coriander spiced crust. Garnish with fresh mint, honey, and berries and enjoy as dessert or any time of the day!

INGREDIENTS

For the crust:

¾ cup Graham cracker crumbs

½ cup unsalted butter, melted

¼ cup granola

¼ cup brown sugar

½ tablespoons poppy seeds

1 teaspoon ground coriander

For the filling:

1 cup cream cheese, softened

½ cup Greek yogurt

1 teaspoon vanilla extract

INSTRUCTIONS

1. Choose 3 (8-oz.) containers; these can be jars or bowls, glass, or plastic.*

2. Combine the Graham cracker crumbs, butter, granola, sugar, poppy seeds, and coriander in a medium bowl.

3. Divide the mixture evenly among the three jars and press into the bottom to form a base.

4. Add the cream cheese, Greek yogurt, and vanilla extract to a medium bowl, stirring to combine.

recipe and ingredients continue

For the topping:

½ cup fresh strawberries, diced

¼ cup fresh blueberries

¼ cup fresh raspberries

2 tablespoons honey

3 fresh mint leaves

5. Pour yogurt mixture over the graham cracker granola crust, cover with a lid or plastic wrap, and chill in the fridge overnight.

6. Before serving, top with the strawberries, blueberries, raspberries, and (optional) honey.

NOTE: *Choose containers with well-fitting lids for an on-the-go breakfast, lunch, or snack.

NUTRITION · PER ONE SERVING

Calories **717 (33%)**

Total Fat **49.38 g (102%)**
  Saturated Fat **30.1 g**
  Polyunsaturated Fat **2.829 g**
  Monounsaturated Fat **13.658 g**
  Trans Fat **0.002 g**

Cholesterol **117 mg**

Sodium **438 mg (29%)**

Total Carbohydrate: **62.04 g (25%)**
  Dietary Fiber: **3.3 g (13%)**
  Total Sugars: **50.47 g**

Protein: **10.84 g (20%)**

Vitamin A **1526 mcg (65%)**

Vitamin C **16.7 mcg (22%)**

Vitamin D **33 mcg (6%)**

Potassium **357 mg (8%)**

Calcium **184 mg (18%)**

Iron **2.48 mg (14%)**

YOGURT AND GRANOLA

Strawberry Coconut Yogurt

Makes 4 servings

PREP TIME: 15 minutes • **COOK TIME:** 12 minutes • **TOTAL TIME:** 27 minutes
Level 2: Easy

Bursting with flavor from the crunchy granola topping, tart strawberries, toasted coconut, and sweet honey, this is an easy dessert to whip up when you're in a time crunch. In fact, it may very well become your go-to dessert for busy nights.

INGREDIENTS

1 cup sweetened coconut flakes

2 cups plain Greek yogurt

2 cups granola

2 cups strawberries, chopped

4 tablespoons honey

INSTRUCTIONS

1. Choose 4 (8-oz.) containers; these can be jars or bowls, glass, or plastic.*

2. Preheat oven to 325°F and line a cookie sheet with parchment paper.

3. Bake the shredded coconut on the prepared cookie sheet for 6 minutes. Toss and bake for an additional 6 minutes, or until golden brown.

4. Divide the yogurt evenly among the 4 bowls, add the granola, and top with the strawberries.

5. (Optional) Sprinkle with the toasted coconut, granola, and drizzle with honey. Serve and enjoy!

NOTE: *Choose containers with well-fitting lids for an on-the-go breakfast, lunch, or snack.

NUTRITION · PER ONE SERVING

Calories **770 (35%)**

Total Fat **29.99 g (62%)**

   Saturated Fat **19.401 g**

   Polyunsaturated Fat **3.159 g**

   Monounsaturated Fat **5.039 g**

   Trans Fat **0 g**

Cholesterol **16 mg**

Sodium **308 mg (21%)**

Total Carbohydrate: **114.71 g (47%)**

   Dietary Fiber: **10 g (40%)**

   Total Sugars: **68.3 g**

Protein: **13.59 g (25%)**

Vitamin A **141 mcg (6%)**

Vitamin C **43.3 mcg (58%)**

Vitamin D **4 mcg (1%)**

Potassium **711 mg (15%)**

Calcium **210 mg (21%)**

Iron **2.53 mg (14%)**

Blueberry Yogurt Granola Jar

Makes 4 servings

PREP TIME: 15 minutes • **COOK TIME:** 1 minute • **TOTAL TIME:** 16 minutes
Level 1: Very Easy

Yes, mustard seeds really are the secret ingredient in this yogurt dessert! The seeds are toasted until fragrant, ground using a mortar and pestle, and sprinkled as the final touch on crunchy granola-topped creamy yogurt. If you prefer a subtle flavor, go for yellow seeds. If you want something more pungent, try brown or black ones!

INGREDIENTS

- 1 teaspoon yellow mustard seeds
- 1 cup Greek yogurt
- ½ cup blueberries
- 1 teaspoon brown sugar
- 1 cup granola

NOTE: *Choose containers with well-fitting lids for an on-the-go breakfast, lunch, or snack.

INSTRUCTIONS

1. Choose 4 (8-oz.) containers; these can be jars or bowls, glass, or plastic.*

2. Cook the mustard seeds in a small, hot skillet set over medium-high heat, until fragrant (30–60 seconds). Transfer immediately to a mortar and pestle and grind the seeds into a fine powder. Set aside.

3. Combine the yogurt, blueberries, and sugar in a medium bowl, mixing well. Divide the mixture between the serving containers.

4. Top with the granola, your favorite fruit, and a sprinkle of the powdered mustard seeds. Serve and enjoy!

NUTRITION • PER ONE SERVING

Calories **195 (9%)**
Total Fat **6.44 g (9%)**
  Saturated Fat **1.598 g**
  Polyunsaturated Fat **1.165 g**
  Monounsaturated Fat **3.298 g**
  Trans Fat **0.04 g**
Cholesterol **7.108 mg (2%)**
Sodium **28.3 mg (2%)**
Total Carbohydrate: **28.24 g (11%)**
  Dietary Fiber: **3.7 g (13%)**
  Total Sugars: **10.95 g (12%)**

Protein: **8.1 g (16%)**
Vitamin A **76.5 mcg (3%)**
Vitamin C **2 mcg (3%)**
Vitamin D **1.7 mcg (0.25%)**
Potassium **101 mg (6%)**
Calcium **101 mg (10%)**
Iron **1 mg (6%)**

Maple Apple Yogurt Jar

Makes 2 servings

PREP TIME: 10 minutes • **COOK TIME:** 0 • **TOTAL TIME:** 1 hour 10 minutes
Level 1: Very Easy

This Maple Apple Yogurt merges luscious maple syrup and tart Granny Smith apples in a perfectly balanced flavor, managing to quench your sweet and sour cravings. In addition to its well-balanced taste, this dish boasts fiber, protein, healthy fats, and essential nutrients.

INGREDIENTS

1 cup plain Greek yogurt

1 Granny Smith apple, cored and diced

2 tablespoons brown sugar

2 tablespoons walnuts, toasted and chopped

2 teaspoons maple syrup

¼ teaspoon ground cinnamon

INSTRUCTIONS

1. Choose 2 (8-oz.) containers; these can be jars or bowls, glass, or plastic.*

2. Add the Greek yogurt, Granny Smith apple, sugar, walnuts, maple syrup, and cinnamons in separate layers to the containers.

3. Cover with the lid or plastic wrap and chill for at least 1 hour before serving, or overnight to serve for breakfast. Enjoy!

NOTE: *Choose containers with well-fitting lids for an on-the-go breakfast, lunch, or snack.

NUTRITION · PER ONE SERVING

Calories **221 (10%)**
Total Fat **8.78 g (18%)**
  Saturated Fat **2.841 g**
  Polyunsaturated Fat **2.956 g**
  Monounsaturated Fat **2.3 g**
  Trans Fat **0 g**
Cholesterol **16 mg**
Sodium **58.5 mg (4%)**
Total Carbohydrate: **30.475 g (12.5%)**
  Dietary Fiber: **3 g (12%)**
  Total Sugars: **25.60 g**

Protein: **6.51 g (12%)**
Vitamin A **209 mcg (9%)**
Vitamin C **0.75 mcg (1%)**
Vitamin D **2.5 mcg (0.5%)**
Potassium **346.5 mg (7.5%)**
Calcium **168 mg (17%)**
Iron **0.47 mg (2.5%)**

Banana Yogurt Granola Jar

Makes 2 servings

PREP TIME: 15 minutes • **COOK TIME:** 0 • Total Time 1 hour 15 minutes
Level 1: Very Easy

Made with only six Ingredients, this simple dessert marinates in the fridge, allowing the flavors to blend. Sweetened with fig jam and studded with fresh banana slices, cherries, and chocolate nibs, you'll wonder why you never experimented with yogurt bowls before.

INGREDIENTS

- 1 cup plain Greek yogurt
- 3 cherries, pitted and chopped
- ½ banana, sliced
- 1 tablespoon granola
- 2 teaspoons fig jam
- 2 teaspoons chocolate nibs

INSTRUCTIONS

1. Choose 2 (8-oz.) containers; these can be jars or bowls, glass, or plastic.*

2. Add the Greek yogurt, cherries, banana, granola, fig jam, and chocolate nibs in separate layers to the containers.

3. Cover with the lid or plastic wrap and chill for at least 1 hour before serving, or overnight to serve for breakfast. Enjoy!

NOTE: *Choose containers with well-fitting lids for an on-the-go breakfast, lunch, or snack.

NUTRITION • PER ONE SERVING

Calories **281 (13%)**
Total Fat **14.03 g (29%)**
  Saturated Fat **8.59 g**
  Polyunsaturated Fat **0.735 g**
  Monounsaturated Fat **3.848 g**
  Trans Fat **0 g**
Cholesterol **16 mg**
Sodium **84 mg (6%)**
Total Carbohydrate: **32.05 g (13%)**
  Dietary Fiber: **4.3 g (17%)**
  Total Sugars: **19.635 g**

Protein: **7.78 g (14%)**
Vitamin A **148 mcg (6.5%)**
Vitamin C **7.75 mcg (10.5%)**
Vitamin D **2.5 mcg (0.5%)**
Potassium **479.5 mg (10%)**
Calcium **173 mg (17.5%)**
Iron **2.905 mg (16%)**

Peach Yogurt Granola Jar

Makes 2 servings

PREP TIME: 15 minutes • **COOK TIME:** 0 • **TOTAL TIME:** 15 minutes
Level 1: Very Easy

This is the perfect dessert for anyone who dreads even thinking about having to make dessert after cooking dinner. When you find yourself in that predicament, this treat will give you back your evening (and you can even make it a day ahead)!

INGREDIENTS

1 cup plain Greek yogurt

1½ tablespoons peach jam

1 cup fresh peach slices

⅓ cup granola

INSTRUCTIONS

1. Choose 2 (8-oz.) containers; these can be jars or bowls, glass, or plastic.*

2. Combine the yogurt and peach jam in a medium bowl, mixing well.

3. Add a layer of peach slices to the bottom of each jar, top with the yogurt mixture, and sprinkle with the granola.

4. Serve immediately or refrigerate for the next day.

NOTE: *Choose containers with well-fitting lids for an on-the-go breakfast, lunch, or snack.

NUTRITION · PER ONE SERVING

Calories **438 (20%)**
Total Fat **16.61 g (34%)**
  Saturated Fat **9.595 g**
  Polyunsaturated Fat **2 g**
  Monounsaturated Fat **3.414 g**
  Trans Fat **0 g**
Cholesterol **16 mg**
Sodium **175 mg (12%)**
Total Carbohydrate: **65.67 g (27%)**
  Dietary Fiber: **5.5 g (22%)**
  Total Sugars: **37.41 g**

Protein: **10.07 g (18%)**
Vitamin A **379 mcg (16%)**
Vitamin C **5.8 mcg (8%)**
Vitamin D **3 mcg (1%)**
Potassium **545 mg (12%)**
Calcium **183 mg (18%)**
Iron **1.4 mg (8%)**

Nut Pomegranate Granola Yogurt Bowl

Makes 4 servings

PREP TIME: 30 minutes • **COOK TIME:** 17 minutes • **TOTAL TIME:** 47 minutes
Level 3: Moderate

This is one of those versatile desserts that can easily double as breakfast or even a light lunch! This truly delightful combination of yogurt topped with chewy almonds, crunchy walnuts, and freshly sliced peaches, is drizzled with energizing pomegranate syrup. Even though you may be tempted to use store-bought pomegranate juice, squeezing your own is really easy!

INGREDIENTS

¾ cup rolled oats

½ cup blanched almonds, roughly chopped

½ cup walnuts, roughly chopped

¼ cup honey, divided

1 tablespoon extra-virgin olive oil

2 pomegranates

1 tablespoon lemon juice, freshly squeezed

2 cups Greek yogurt

2 peaches, sliced

INSTRUCTIONS

1. Choose 4 (8-oz.) containers; these can be jars or bowls, glass, or plastic.*

2. Preheat oven to 325°F and line a cookie sheet with parchment paper.

3. Combine the oats, almonds, walnuts, 2 tablespoons of the honey, and olive oil in a bowl, mixing well, until the honey evenly coats the nuts.

4. Arrange the granola in a single layer on the prepared cookie sheet and bake for 8 minutes. Turn over granola and bake for an additional 7 minutes.

5. Allow granola to cool on the pan and when completely cool, break it into small pieces.

6. Cut the pomegranates in half, and set aside one half.

7. Juice the one pomegranate half with a lemon squeezer and allow juice to run through a fine-mesh strainer set over a small saucepan.

recipe continues

8. Add the lemon juice and the remaining honey to the pomegranate juice. Bring the mixture to a boil over medium-high heat and continue cooking for 2 minutes. Remove from heat and cool completely.

9. Remove the seeds from the reserved pomegranate half and stir into the cooled syrup, set aside.

10. Divide the Greek yogurt evenly among the 4 bowls, top with pomegranate syrup or fresh pomegranate seeds.

11. Serve immediately or refrigerate for the next day.

NOTE: *Choose containers with well-fitting lids for an on-the-go breakfast, lunch, or snack.

NUTRITION · PER ONE SERVING

Calories **492 (23%)**
Total Fat **22.73 g (47%)**
  Saturated Fat **4.569 g**
  Polyunsaturated Fat **8.875 g**
  Monounsaturated Fat **6.991 g**
  Trans Fat **0.02 g**
Cholesterol **16 mg**
Sodium **62 mg (4%)**
Total Carbohydrate: **72.48 g (29%)**
  Dietary Fiber: **11.6 g (46%)**
  Total Sugars: **49.8 g**

Protein: **4.37 g (26%)**
Vitamin A **368 mcg (16%)**
Vitamin C **21.7 mcg (29%)**
Vitamin D **2 mcg**
Potassium **908 mg (19%)**
Calcium **219 mg (22%)**
Iron **2.44 mg (14%)**

Orange Yogurt Granola

Makes 4 servings

PREP TIME: 25 minutes • **COOK TIME:** 30 minutes • **TOTAL TIME:** 55 minutes
Level 3: Moderate

Carob molasses really Makes this dessert yogurt stand out, and it's easily made (as you'll see in the recipe) using a delightful carob spread available from any Middle Eastern market. If you question the extra effort, trust me, you'll forget all about it after one spoonful.

INGREDIENTS

- 1½ cups quick-cooking oats
- 1 cup walnuts, chopped
- 1 cup orange juice, freshly squeezed
- ½ cup almonds, sliced
- ¼ cup sunflower seeds
- 1½ teaspoons ground cinnamon
- 3 tablespoons canola oil
- 2 tablespoons honey
- 1½ teaspoons vanilla extract
- ½ cup dried cranberries
- 1 cup Greek yogurt
- 2 tablespoons carob molasses

INSTRUCTIONS

1. Choose 4 (8-oz.) containers; these can be jars or bowls, glass, or plastic.*

2. Preheat oven to 350°F and line a cookie sheet with parchment paper.

3. Combine the oats, walnuts, orange juice, almonds, sunflower seeds, and cinnamon in a large bowl, mixing well.

4. Whisk together the canola oil, honey, and vanilla extract in a separate bowl, then add it to the oat mixture, stirring until well coated.

5. Spread the granola mixture evenly on the prepared cookie sheet and bake for 30 minutes, stirring every 10 minutes, until the granola turns a golden brown.

6. Remove the cookie sheet from the oven, mix in the cranberries, then allow everything to cool completely.

recipe continues

7. Whisk together the yogurt and carob molasses in a medium bowl. Mix in the cooled granola and divide among the 4 containers.

8. Serve immediately or refrigerate for the next day.

NOTE: *Choose containers with well-fitting lids for an on-the-go breakfast, lunch, or snack.

NUTRITION · PER ONE SERVING

Calories **591 (27%)**
Total Fat **40.02 g (82%)**
  Saturated Fat **4.521 g**
  Polyunsaturated Fat **17.083 g**
  Monounsaturated Fat **16.536 g**
  Trans Fat **0.044 g**
Cholesterol **8 mg**
Sodium **36 mg (2%)**
Total Carbohydrate: **56.63 g (23%)**
  Dietary Fiber: **8 g (32%)**
  Total Sugars: **35.96 g**

Protein: **13.92 g (25%)**
Vitamin A **196 mcg (8%)**
Vitamin C **31.8 mcg (42%)**
Vitamin D **1 mcg**
Potassium **735 mg (16%)**
Calcium **196 mg (20%)**
Iron **3.26 mg (18%)**

YOGURT AND GRANOLA

Snacks

Lemon-Mint Pesto Tartines

Makes 10 servings

PREP TIME: 35 minutes • **COOK TIME:** 10 minutes • **TOTAL TIME:** 45 minutes
Level 2: Easy

Tartines are open sandwiches, and they date back to the 1400s when thin slices of bread served as plates! This modern take slathers freshly blended lemon-mint pesto onto toasted bread topped with juicy blueberries.

INGREDIENTS

½ medium lemon, seeded and sliced into ½-inch thick rounds

¼ cup + 3 tablespoons extra-virgin olive oil, divided

1 cup fresh mint leaves, packed

¼ cup almonds, toasted*

¼ teaspoon salt

1 small loaf sourdough bread or a baguette, sliced and toasted

12 ounces whole milk ricotta cheese

2 cups fresh blueberries

INSTRUCTIONS

1. Preheat oven to 450°F.

2. Arrange lemon slices on a half cookie sheet, drizzle with 1 tablespoon of olive oil and bake for 5–10 minutes, until the lemons caramelize.

3. Cool the lemon slices for 10 minutes before transferring them to the bowl of a food processor. Add the remaining olive oil, mint, almonds, and salt and process until it forms a slightly chunky pesto.

4. Before serving, spread each slice of bread with ricotta cheese and top with pesto and 5–6 blueberries. Refrigerate leftovers in an airtight container for up to 3 days.

NOTE: *Hazelnuts also work beautifully if you'd like to substitute them for the almonds.

NUTRITION · PER ONE SERVING

Calories **423 (19%)**
Total Fat **16.43 g (34%)**
  Saturated Fat **4.642 g**
  Polyunsaturated Fat **2.062 g**
  Monounsaturated Fat **8.505 g**
  Trans Fat **0.009 g**
Cholesterol **17 mg**
Sodium **665 mg (44%)**
Total Carbohydrate: **55 g (22%)**
  Dietary Fiber: **4.3 g (17%)**
  Total Sugars: **6.53 g**

Protein: **14.91 g (27%)**
Vitamin A **396 mcg (17%)**
Vitamin C **10.3 mcg (14%)**
Vitamin D **3 mcg (1%)**
Potassium **222 mg (5%)**
Calcium **136 mg (14%)**
Iron **4.27 mg (24%)**

Lebanese Dried Apricot Spread

Makes 6 servings

PREP TIME: 12 minutes • **COOK TIME:** 0 • **TOTAL TIME:** 12 minutes
Level 2: Easy

Kashta is a delectably rich and creamy Middle Eastern treat that is also referred to as Lebanese ricotta cheese. Loaded with healthy fats, kashta is commonly served cold with honey in addition to being an ingredient used in cooking. Here we are mixing it up with nuts and fruit as a tasty spread.

INGREDIENTS

- 12 dried apricots
- 1 avocado, sliced
- 1 cup kashta
- 2 tablespoons mixed nuts, crushed
- 3 tablespoons honey

INSTRUCTIONS

1. Arrange the dried apricots and avocado slices onto a serving platter or dessert dish and top with the kashta. Sprinkle with the mixed nuts and drizzle with honey.

2. Top your favorite bread, toast, crepes, or pita bread with this Lebanese Dried Apricot Spread, if desired. Refrigerate leftovers in an airtight container for up to 3 days.

NUTRITION • PER ONE SERVING

Calories **237 (11%)**
Total Fat **6.37 g (13%)**
  Saturated Fat **0.864 g**
  Polyunsaturated Fat **1.003 g**
  Monounsaturated Fat **3.936 g**
  Trans Fat **0 g**
Cholesterol **0 mg**
Sodium **8 mg (1%)**
Total Carbohydrate: **47.73 g (19%)**
  Dietary Fiber: **6.7 g (27%)**
  Total Sugars: **39.34 g**

Protein: **3.14 g (6%)**
Vitamin A **2103 mcg (90%)**
Vitamin C **4.1 mcg (5%)**
Vitamin D **0 mcg**
Potassium **853 mg (18%)**
Calcium **39 mg (4%)**
Iron **1.84 mg (10%)**

Mouloukhiye Yogurt Dip

Makes 16 servings

PREP TIME: 20 minutes • **COOK TIME:** 35 minutes • **TOTAL TIME:** 55 minutes
Level 3: Moderate

Mouloukhiye, also known as Mulukhiyah, molokheyya, molokhia, or mulukhiyyah, is a traditional Middle Eastern stew that contains jute mallow leaves. In this dip version, we're taking a shortcut and using the frozen version mixed with yogurt and three different cheeses. Expect a round of applause from your guests thanks to this exotic and versatile recipe.

INGREDIENTS

1 (10-oz.) package frozen Mouloukhiye, thawed

1½ cups plain Greek yogurt

1 cup feta, crumbled

⅔ cups + 4 tablespoons mozzarella, shredded, and divided

⅓ cup + 4 tablespoons parmesan, shredded, and divided

2 garlic cloves, minced

INSTRUCTIONS

1. Preheat oven to 350°F and coat a 9-×-13-inch baking dish with non-stick cooking spray.

2. Remove the liquid from the thawed Mouloukhiye by placing it in a clean tea towel or cheesecloth and squeezing or pressing it into a fine-mesh strainer set over a sink or bowl.

3. Combine the Mouloukhiye in a medium bowl with the Greek yogurt, feta, ⅔ cup of the mozzarella, ⅓ cup of the parmesan, and garlic, mixing well.

4. Transfer the mixture into the prepared casserole dish and top with the remaining 4 tablespoons of mozzarella and 4 tablespoons of parmesan.

5. Bake for 30–35 minutes, until heated through and the cheese is golden brown.

6. Serve hot with your favorite chips, crackers, or freshly cut veggies. Refrigerate leftovers in an airtight container for up to 3 days.

NUTRITION • PER ONE SERVING

Calories **114 (19.34%)**
Total Fat **2.49 g (5%)**
  Saturated Fat **1.704 g**
  Polyunsaturated Fat **0.072 g**
  Monounsaturated Fat **0.545 g**
  Trans Fat **0.001 g**
Cholesterol **17 mg**
Sodium **384 mg (8%)**
Total Carbohydrate **5.66 g (2%)**
  Dietary Fiber **0.9 g (2%)**
  Total Sugars **1.69 g**

Protein: **16.35 g (29%)**
Vitamin A **769 mcg (11%)**
Vitamin C **0.1 mcg**
Vitamin D **9.2 mcg**
Potassium **90 mg (2%)**
Calcium **417 mg (42%)**
Iron **0.34 mg (2%)**

Halloumi Spinach Green Pepper Balls

Makes 12 servings

PREP TIME: 30 minutes • **COOK TIME:** 25 minutes • **TOTAL TIME:** 55 minutes
Level 3: Moderate

Crumbled, tangy halloumi cheese, earthy spinach, and diced bell peppers are folded into a savory, yet sweet dough and baked to golden perfection. Serve these on a platter of afternoon delights or for a rushed breakfast. Either way, they'll disappear faster than you made them!

INGREDIENTS

2¾ cups all-purpose flour

¼ cup granulated sugar

2 teaspoons baking powder

1 teaspoon ground paprika

¾ teaspoon salt

¾ cup low-fat milk

½ cup extra-virgin olive oil

2 large eggs

1¼ cups fresh spinach, minced

¾ cup Halloumi cheese, crumbled

⅓ cup green bell pepper, diced

INSTRUCTIONS

1. Preheat oven to 375°F and line a cookie sheet with parchment paper.

2. Whisk together the flour, granulated sugar, baking powder, paprika, and salt in a large bowl.

3. Whisk together the milk, olive oil, and eggs in a separate medium bowl, then add to dry Ingredients, mixing until combined.

4. Fold in the spinach, Halloumi cheese, and green pepper.

5. Scoop rounded tablespoons of batter onto the prepared cookie sheet, leaving 1-inch spaces between each.

6. Bake 25 minutes, until a toothpick inserted in the center comes out clean.

7. Cool on the pan for 10 minutes, then transfer to a wire rack to cool completely.

8. Serve at room temperature. Refrigerate leftovers in an airtight container for up to 3 days.

NUTRITION · PER ONE SERVING

Calories **245 (11%)**
Total Fat **12.92 g (27%)**
  Saturated Fat **3.32 g**
  Polyunsaturated Fat **1.333 g**
  Monounsaturated Fat **7.707 g**
  Trans Fat **0.02 g**
Cholesterol **40 mg**
Sodium **218 mg (15%)**
Total Carbohydrate: **25.51 g (10%)**
  Dietary Fiber: **1 g (4%)**
  Total Sugars: **3.05 g**

Protein: **6.67 g (12%)**
Vitamin A **534 mcg (23%)**
Vitamin C **2.9 mcg (4%)**
Vitamin D **16 mcg (3%)**
Potassium **181 mg (4%)**
Calcium **129 mg (13%)**
Iron **1.79 mg (10%)**

Lentil Dip

Makes 6 servings

PREP TIME: 12 minutes • **COOK TIME:** 20 minutes • **TOTAL TIME:** 32 minutes
Level 2: Easy

Is doesn't matter if you use earthy brown lentils, peppery green lentils, or sweet red lentils; you'll still reap all the health benefits of this amazing legume, including improved digestion. This dip, seasoned with flavorful and fragrant spices, is as tempting as it is healthy.

INGREDIENTS

1 cup lentils,* picked over and rinsed

2 teaspoons curry powder

1 teaspoon onion powder

1 teaspoon sea salt

¼ teaspoon black pepper

¼ teaspoon turmeric

½ teaspoon ground cumin

INSTRUCTIONS

1. Cook the lentils according to package directions, drain well, and place in a medium bowl.

2. Mash the cooked lentils with a fork until a paste forms.

3. Stir in the curry powder, onion powder, salt, black pepper, turmeric, and cumin.

4. Serve in a decorative bowl along with crackers or pita bread, if desired. Refrigerate leftovers in an airtight container for up to 3 days.

NOTE: *All types of lentils work well in this lentil dip.

NUTRITION · PER ONE SERVING

Calories **19 (1%)**

Total Fat **0.22 g**
  Saturated Fat **0.026 g**
  Polyunsaturated Fat **0.058 g**
  Monounsaturated Fat **0.1 g**
  Trans Fat **0 g**
Cholesterol **0 mg**
Sodium **390 mg (26%)**
Total Carbohydrate: **3.78 g (2%)**
  Dietary Fiber: **0.7 g (3%)**
  Total Sugars: **0.05 g**

Protein: **1.34 g (2%)**
Vitamin A **9 mcg**
Vitamin C **2.2 mcg (3%)**
Vitamin D **0 mcg**
Potassium **61 mg (1%)**
Calcium **11 mg (1%)**
Iron **0.76 mg (4%)**

Beet Chips

Makes 8 servings

PREP TIME: 15 minutes • **COOK TIME:** 45 minutes • **TOTAL TIME:** 55 minutes

Level 3: Moderate

Everyone seems to have a love-hate relationship with potato chips, so what if I told you that you could fall in love with a healthy version that tastes just as good, and will satisfy your chip craving? These Beet Chips are that chip. Crunchy, salty, and just a tad sweet, they're perfect for when you're in a snacking mood.

INGREDIENTS

10 medium beets*

¼ cup olive oil

1 tablespoon chives, chopped

1 teaspoon sea salt

NOTES: *For variety, experiment with different color beets, or cook up a combination of colors.

**If you do not have a mandolin, thinly slice the beets using a knife.

INSTRUCTIONS

1. Preheat oven to 300°F and line a cookie sheet with parchment paper

2. Trim the beets and cut them into very thin slices using a mandolin.**

3. Arrange the beet slices side by side on the cookie sheet in an even layer, and sprinkle with olive oil.

4. Bake the chips for 45 minutes, turning them over halfway through.

5. Let the chips cool completely then sprinkle them with the chives and salt. Serve immediately. Store leftovers in an airtight container for up to 5 days.

NUTRITION • PER ONE SERVING

Calories **84 (4%)**

Total Fat **7.22 g (10%)**

   Saturated Fat **1.00 g (5%)**

   Polyunsaturated Fat **0.78 g**

   Monounsaturated Fat **5.021 g**

   Trans Fat **0 g**

Cholesterol **0 mg**

Sodium **275 mg (14%)**

Total Carbohydrate: **10.82 g (5%)**

   Dietary Fiber: **2.9 g (12%)**

   Total Sugars: **6.94 g**

Protein: **1.66 g (3%)**

Vitamin A **55 mcg (2%)**

Vitamin C **5.2 mcg (7%)**

Vitamin D **0 mcg**

Potassium **350 mg (8%)**

Calcium **20 mg (3%)**

Iron **0.83 mg (5%)**

Navy Bean Dip

Makes 7 servings

PREP TIME: 20 minutes • **COOK TIME:** 3 minutes • **TOTAL TIME:** 23 minutes
Level 3: Moderate

Besides being one of nature's most healthful foods, navy beans—which are white, not navy—are known for their nutty, earthy flavor, which Makes them perfect to use in dips. Flavored with delicious garlic-infused oil and seasoned to perfection, this dip is equally enjoyed with raw vegetables or crispy pita chips.

INGREDIENTS

½ cup olive oil

2 garlic cloves, coarsely chopped

2 (16-oz.) cans navy beans, drained and rinsed

¼ cup lemon juice, freshly squeezed

2 tablespoons parsley, freshly minced

½ tablespoon kosher salt

1 teaspoon white pepper

1 teaspoon ground cumin

¼ teaspoon cayenne pepper

INSTRUCTIONS

1. Pour the olive oil into a small skillet set over medium-low heat, add garlic, and cook for 2–3 minutes, until golden. Remove from heat.

2. Remove the garlic pieces from the olive oil and place onto a small plate. Set both aside to cool.

3. Add the garlic pieces, beans, lemon juice, parsley, salt, white pepper, cumin, and cayenne to the bowl of a food processor, blending until a smooth hummus-like mixture is reached.

4. With the processor still running, gradually add the garlic oil and continue to process until the dip is light and smooth.

5. Serve with cut up raw vegetables or pita chips. Refrigerate leftovers in an airtight container for up to 3 days.

NUTRITION · PER ONE SERVING

Calories **237 (11%)**
Total Fat **16.53 g (34%)**
　Saturated Fat **2.264 g**
　Polyunsaturated Fat **2.215 g**
　Monounsaturated Fat **11.38 g**
　Trans Fat **0.007 g**
Cholesterol **0 mg**
Sodium **804 mg (54%)**
Total Carbohydrate: **1.96 g (8%)**
　Dietary Fiber: **0.2 g (1%)**
Total Sugars: **0.25 g**

Protein: **8.8 g (16%)**
Vitamin A **130 mcg (6%)**
Vitamin C **26.3 mcg (35%)**
Vitamin D **0 mcg**
Potassium **411 mg (9%)**
Calcium **27 mg (3%)**
Iron **3 mg (17%)**

Tomato Bites

Makes 20 servings

PREP TIME: 20 minutes • **COOK TIME:** 18 minutes • **TOTAL TIME:** 38 minutes
Level 2: Easy

Save this recipe for when your garden tomatoes ripen—you won't regret it! You can even use homegrown basil and oregano. This flaky, buttery puff pastry is topped with rich, nutty Gouda, acidic plum tomatoes, tangy olives, and salty feta cheese. Serve these Tomato Bites as an appetizer or an afternoon snack.

INGREDIENTS

- 1 (8-oz.) package of frozen puff pastry, thawed (1 sheet)
- 1½ cups Gouda cheese, shredded
- 6 plum tomatoes, thinly sliced
- 1 cup feta cheese, crumble
- ¼ cup pitted Kalamata olives, coarsely chopped
- 3 tablespoons basil, freshly minced
- 3 tablespoons oregano, freshly minced

INSTRUCTIONS

1. Preheat oven to 400°F and line a cookie sheet with parchment paper.

2. Unfold the puff pastry and cut into 16 squares. Arrange pastry squares on the prepared cookie sheet.

3. Sprinkle the pastry squares with the Gouda cheese and top with tomato slices, feta, and olives.

4. Bake for 14–18 minutes, until golden brown.

5. Garnish with basil and oregano and serve warm. Refrigerate leftovers in an airtight container for up to 3 days.

NUTRITION • PER ONE SERVING

Calories **188 (9%)**
Total Fat **13.47 g (28%)**
  Saturated Fat **5.232 g**
  Polyunsaturated Fat **1.282 g**
  Monounsaturated Fat **6.253 g**
  Trans Fat **0 g**
Cholesterol **15 mg**
Sodium **198 mg (13%)**
Total Carbohydrate: **11.75 g (5%)**
  Dietary Fiber: **0.8 g (3%)**
  Total Sugars: **1.03 g**

Protein: **5.38 g (10%)**
Vitamin A **298 mcg (13%)**
Vitamin C **2.6 mcg (3%)**
Vitamin D **3 mcg (1%)**
Potassium **78 mg (2%)**
Calcium **124 mg (12%)**
Iron **0.98 mg (5%)**

Bocconcini Tomato Mini Tart

Makes 4 servings

PREP TIME: 20 minutes • **COOK TIME:** 20 minutes • **TOTAL TIME:** 40 minutes

Level 3: Moderate

The mini mozzarella cheese balls, known as Bocconcini, star in this recipe. When combined with tomatoes, anchovies, and olives, stuffed into a flaky puff pastry shell, these flavorful tarts are the perfect rustic centerpiece for al fresco dining!

INGREDIENTS

- 1 cup tomatoes (preferably plum tomatoes), finely chopped*
- 6 green olives, pitted and roughly chopped
- 4 bocconcini
- 4 anchovies
- 1 tablespoon capers
- 12 basil leaves, roughly torn
- 1 teaspoon salt
- ½ teaspoon black pepper
- 2 sheets puff pastry, thawed and cut into 1-inch circles
- 3 eggs, lightly beaten
- 2 teaspoons black sesame seeds
- 2 tablespoons chives, freshly chopped
- 2 tablespoons parsley, freshly minced
- 2 tablespoons olive oil

INSTRUCTIONS

1. Preheat oven to 425°F and line a cookie sheet with parchment paper.

2. Combine the tomatoes, olives, and bocconcini in a medium bowl. Once mixed, stir in the anchovies, capers, basil leaves, salt, and pepper.

3. Place the circles of puff pastry on the prepared cookie sheet and place a spoonful of the tomato filling on the center of each.

4. Lightly brush the edge of the tarts with the beaten eggs and pinch to create a decorative border. Finish with a sprinkle of black sesame seeds if desire.

5. Bake tarts for 15–20 minutes, until golden.

6. Garnish with chives, parsley, and olive oil. Serve warm.

NOTE: *Plum tomatoes work best with these Bocconcini Tomato Mini Tarts as they provide a much-needed acidic kick that perfectly complements the salty anchovies and tangy olives.

NUTRITION · PER ONE SERVING

Calories **764 (35%)**
Total Fat **55.06 g (113%)**
  Saturated Fat **13.578 g**
  Polyunsaturated Fat **7.438 g**
  Monounsaturated Fat **31.578 g**
  Trans Fat **0.016 g**
Cholesterol **126 mg**
Sodium **1175 mg (78%)**
Total Carbohydrate: **53.68 g (22%)**
  Dietary Fiber: **2.7 g (11%)**
  Total Sugars: **2.02 g**

Protein: **14.42 g (26%)**
Vitamin A **742 mcg (32%)**
Vitamin C **8.6 mcg (11%)**
Vitamin D **30 mcg (5%)**
Potassium **253 mg (5%)**
Calcium **53 mg (5%)**
Iron **4.13 mg (23%)**

Savory Sun-Dried Olive Biscuits

Makes 12 biscuits

PREP TIME: 35 minutes • **COOK TIME:** 30 minutes • **TOTAL TIME:** 1 hour 5 minutes
Level 3: Moderate

These Mediterranean-inspired biscuits are loaded with zesty sun-dried tomatoes, tangy olives, and fragrant garlic, all coated in a delicate chickpea flour batter. Dip these snacks in your favorite sauces or nibble them on their own when you're on-the-go.

INGREDIENTS

1 teaspoon olive oil + ½ cup olive oil, divided

1 large onion, chopped

4 garlic cloves, minced

¾ cup sun-dried tomatoes in oil, drained and chopped

⅔ cup green olives, chopped and pitted

1⅓ cups all-purpose flour

1⅓ cups chickpea flour

2 teaspoons baking powder

½ teaspoon salt

1 teaspoon dried basil

1 teaspoon dried oregano

1 teaspoon dried parsley

1 teaspoon dried thyme

1 cup cold water

1½ teaspoons apple cider vinegar

INSTRUCTIONS

1. Place the teaspoon of olive oil in a skillet set over medium-high heat. Add the chopped onions and minced garlic, cooking for 3–4 minutes, until the onions soften and start to brown.

2. Add the sun-dried tomatoes and olives, cook for 1 minute, then remove pan from the heat and let it cool.

3. Preheat oven to 400°F and line a cookie sheet with parchment paper.

4. Whisk together the all-purpose flour, chickpea flour, baking powder, and salt in a large bowl. Add the basil, oregano, parsley, and thyme.

5. Add the ½ cup olive oil, water, and apple cider vinegar, whisking until the batter is mostly smooth with a few clumps.

6. Gently fold the sundried tomato mixture into the batter.

7. Dollop tablespoons of batter onto the prepared cookie sheet, leaving 1-inch spaces between them.

8. Bake for 22–25 minutes, until golden.

9. Cool biscuits for 10 minutes on the pan before transferring to a wire rack to cool completely. Serve and enjoy! Refrigerate leftovers in an airtight container for up to 3 days.

NUTRITION · PER ONE SERVING

Calories **90 (9%)**

Total Fat **10.35 g (21%)**
   Saturated Fat **1.414 g**
   Polyunsaturated Fat **1.395 g**
   Monounsaturated Fat **7.042 g**
   Trans Fat **0.004 g**

Cholesterol **0 mg**

Sodium **117 mg (8%)**

Total Carbohydrate: **20.36 g (8%)**
   Dietary Fiber: **2.2 g (9%)**
   Total Sugars: **2.96 g**

Protein: **4.42 g (8%)**

Vitamin A **49 mcg (2%)**

Vitamin C **2.8 mcg (4%)**

Vitamin D **0 mcg**

Potassium **327 mg (7%)**

Calcium **56 mg (6%)**

Iron **1.71 mg (10%)**

Feta Blueberry Duck Scones

Makes 12 scones

PREP TIME: 45 minutes • **COOK TIME:** 15 minutes • **TOTAL TIME:** 1 hour
Level 4: Challenging

Snacks aren't always sweet, and these Feta Blueberry Duck Scones are a delicious example! Each flaky scone is studded with juicy blueberries, salty feta, and bits of smoked duck breast. Loaded with protein, this snack is guaranteed to keep you satisfied until your next meal!

INGREDIENTS

For the scones:

¾ cups + 3 tablespoons self-rising flour

½ cup + 1 tablespoon whole wheat flour

¼ teaspoon baking powder

¼ teaspoon cayenne pepper

¼ teaspoon mustard powder

⅓ cup feta cheese, cubed

¼ cup smoked duck breast, chopped

10 Kalamata olives, pitted and chopped

1½ teaspoons thyme, chopped

1 large egg

2 tablespoons milk

2 tablespoons extra-virgin olive oil

¼ cup dried cranberries

INSTRUCTIONS

1. Preheat oven to 350°F and line a cookie sheet with parchment paper.

To make the scones:

1. Whisk the self-rising flour, whole wheat flour, baking powder, cayenne pepper, and mustard powder in a large bowl. Stir in the feta, duck breast, olives, and thyme.

2. Whisk together the egg, milk, and olive oil in a small bowl, then add half of it to the dry Ingredients.

3. Mix until a soft dough forms, adding more egg and milk mixture, as needed. Once the dough is the right consistency, fold in the cranberries and blueberries.

4. Turn dough onto a floured surface, roll to 1-inch in thickness. Cut into triangular scone shape.

To make the topping:

1. Arrange scones on the prepared cookie sheet and brush with any remaining milk and egg mixture. Top scones with the crumbled feta.

2. Bake for 12–15 minutes, until golden brown.

3. Cool scones on the pan for 10 minutes then transfer to a wire rack to cool completely.

¼ cup fresh or frozen blueberries

For the topping:

2 tablespoons milk

¼ cup feta cheese, crumbled

4. Serve warm. Refrigerate leftovers in an airtight container for up to 3 days.

NUTRITION · PER ONE SERVING

Calories **118 (5%)**
Total Fat **5.48 g (11%)**
  Saturated Fat **1.856 g**
  Polyunsaturated Fat **0.586 g**
  Monounsaturated Fat **2.724 g**
  Trans Fat **0.001 g**
Cholesterol **29 mg**
Sodium **216 mg (14%)**
Total Carbohydrate: **12.98 g (5%)**
  Dietary Fiber: **1.2 g (5%)**
  Total Sugars: **1.15 g**

Protein: **4.42 g (8%)**
Vitamin A **98 mcg (4%)**
Vitamin C **0.5 mcg (1%)**
Vitamin D **4 mcg (1%)**
Potassium **61 mg (1%)**
Calcium **87 mg (9%)**
Iron **1.07 mg (6%)**

Drinks/Smoothies

Watermelon Rosewater Refresher

Makes 6 servings

PREP TIME: 12 minutes • **COOK TIME:** 0 • **TOTAL TIME:** 12 minutes

Level 1: Very Easy

This bright drink will not only refresh you on summer afternoons, it will make you forget all about lemonade! Crafted with sweet watermelon, tart lemon juice, and savory basil, this drink boasts hints of mint, rose, and anise—creating a flavorful combination that feels as though you're vacationing in the Mediterranean.

INGREDIENTS

- 6 cups ripe watermelon, cubed
- ½ cup fresh basil leaves, loosely packed
- ¼ cup fresh mint leaves, packed
- 3 tablespoons rosewater
- 1 tablespoon fresh lemon juice
- ¼ teaspoon ground star anise

INSTRUCTIONS

1. Combine all Ingredients in a blender and process until smooth.

2. Serve in ice-filled glasses garnished with a fresh basil leaf.

NUTRITION • PER ONE SERVING

Calories **47 (2%)**	Protein: **0.95 g (2%)**
Total Fat **0.24 g**	Vitamin A **879 mcg (38%)**
Saturated Fat **0.026 g**	Vitamin C **13.5 mcg (18%)**
Polyunsaturated Fat **0.078 g**	Vitamin D **0 mcg**
Monounsaturated Fat **0.057 g**	Potassium **178 mg (4%)**
Trans Fat **0 g**	Calcium **12 mg (1%)**
Cholesterol **0 mg**	Iron **0.37 mg (2%)**
Sodium **2 mg**	
Total Carbohydrate: **11.8 g (5%)**	
Dietary Fiber: **0.2 g (2%)**	
Total Sugars: **9.61 g**	

Coconut Blueberry Smoothie

Makes 4 servings

PREP TIME: 12 minutes • **COOK TIME:** 0 • **TOTAL TIME:** 12 minutes
Level 1: Very Easy

Coconut, blueberries, and turmeric are as tasty a combination as they are healthy! These superfoods boast antioxidants and countless vitamins, refreshing not only your tastebuds, but also your health.

INGREDIENTS

- 1 cup coconut milk, chilled
- 1 cup frozen blueberries
- ½ cup plain Greek yogurt
- 1 tablespoon fresh ginger, peeled and grated
- 1 tablespoon turmeric
- 1 tablespoon honey

INSTRUCTIONS

1. Combine all Ingredients in a blender and process until smooth.
2. Serve in ice-filled glasses.

NUTRITION · PER ONE SERVING

Calories **174 (8%)**
Total Fat **13.38 g (28%)**
  Saturated Fat **11.396 g**
  Polyunsaturated Fat **0.288 g**
  Monounsaturated Fat **0.834 g**
  Trans Fat **0.1 g**
Cholesterol **4 mg**
Sodium **23 mg (2%)**
Total Carbohydrate: **13.9 g (6%)**
  Dietary Fiber: **1.6 g (6%)**
  Total Sugars: **9.11 g**

Protein: **2.64 g (5%)**
Vitamin A **48 mcg (2%)**
Vitamin C **1.8 mcg (2%)**
Vitamin D **1 mcg**
Potassium **251 mg (5%)**
Calcium **55 mg (6%)**
Iron **3.27 mg (18%)**

Asparagus Blueberry Drink

Makes 2 servings

PREP TIME: 5 minutes • **COOK TIME:** 0 • **TOTAL TIME:** 35 minutes

Level 1: Very Easy

If you're new to the experience of blending asparagus into a drink, you're not alone! Once you try it though, you'll make it again and again. Asparagus' health benefits include aiding digestion by encouraging healthy gut bacteria. The added vanilla, banana, and fresh dates create a flavorful experience.

INGREDIENTS

- 1½ cups fresh blueberries
- 1 cup asparagus spears, chopped
- 1 banana
- 4 fresh dates, pitted
- 1 teaspoon vanilla extract
- 1 tablespoon chia seeds

INSTRUCTIONS

1. Combine all Ingredients, except the chia seeds, in a blender and process until smooth.
2. Refrigerate for at least 30 minutes, until cool.
3. Pour into two ice-filled glasses and top each with half the chia seeds before serving (optional).

NUTRITION · PER ONE SERVING

Calories **210 (10%)**

Total Fat **2.88 g (6%)**
  Saturated Fat **0.365 g**
  Polyunsaturated Fat **1.922 g**
  Monounsaturated Fat **0.24 g**
  Trans Fat **0.01 g**

Cholesterol **0 mg**

Sodium **5 mg**

Total Carbohydrate: **46.07 g (19%)**
  Dietary Fiber: **9.2 g (37%)**
  Total Sugars: **28.79 g**

Protein: **4.46 g (8%)**

Vitamin A **0 mcg**

Vitamin C **19.8 mg (25%)**

Vitamin D **0 mcg**

Potassium **559 mg (12%)**

Calcium **79 mg (8%)**

Iron **2.62 mg (10%)**

Avocado Coconut Smoothie

Makes 2 servings

PREP TIME: 5 minutes • **COOK TIME:** 0 • **TOTAL TIME:** 35 minutes
Level 1: Very Easy

Avocados have a naturally creamy texture that transform smoothies into luxurious beverages. Drink this for breakfast and the healthy fats from the coconut milk and avocado will keep you satisfied until your next meal!

INGREDIENTS

- 1 cup coconut milk, chilled
- ¼ cup fresh mint leaves, chopped and loosely packed
- ½ avocado
- 3 celery stalks, roughly chopped
- Juice of 1 lime
- 1 teaspoon linseed oil

INSTRUCTIONS

1. Combine all Ingredients, except linseed oil, in a blender and process until smooth.
2. Refrigerate for at least 30 minutes, until cool.
3. Pour into two glasses and top each with ½ teaspoon of linseed oil before serving.

NUTRITION • PER ONE SERVING

- Calories **323 (15%)**
- Total Fat **32.28 g (67%)**
  - Saturated Fat **22.517 g**
  - Polyunsaturated Fat **1.689 g**
  - Monounsaturated Fat **6.689 g**
  - *Trans* Fat **0 g**
- Cholesterol **0 mg**
- Sodium **40 mg (3%)**
- Total Carbohydrate: **10.78 g (4%)**
  - Dietary Fiber: **4.4 g (18%)**
  - Total Sugars: **1.07 g**
- Protein: **4.12 g (8%)**
- Vitamin A **399 mcg (17%)**
- Vitamin C **14.9 mcg (20%)**
- Vitamin D **0 mcg**
- Potassium **607 mg (13%)**
- Calcium **49 mg (5%)**
- Iron **4.28 mg (24%)**

Beet Mango Ginger Smoothie

Makes 2 servings

PREP TIME: 12 minutes • **COOK TIME:** 0 • **TOTAL TIME:** 12 minutes
Level 1: Very Easy

The earthy flavor of beets merges with the sweetness of mangoes and a zing of spicy ginger, crafting this ridiculously healthy and undeniably delicious smoothie. If you're in a crunch for time, whip this up for breakfast the night before. Just make sure you stir before serving!

INGREDIENTS

- 2 cups mango, diced
- 1½ cups almond milk, chilled
- 1 cup frozen blueberries
- 2 small beets, peeled and roughly chopped
- 2 carrots, peeled and roughly chopped
- 3 dates, pitted
- 2 tablespoons ginger, peeled and grated

INSTRUCTIONS

1. Combine all Ingredients in a blender and process until smooth.
2. Pour into two glasses to serve.

NOTE: If the smoothie is too thick, add more almond milk. If the smoothie is too thin, add more mangoes or blueberries, or try adding ice.

NUTRITION • PER ONE SERVING

Calories **301 (14%)**
Total Fat **1.58 g (3%)**
  Saturated Fat **0.45 g**
  Polyunsaturated Fat **0.37 g**
  Monounsaturated Fat **0.401 g**
  Trans Fat **0 g**
Cholesterol **4 mg**
Sodium **206 mg (14%)**
Total Carbohydrate: **67.16 g (27%)**
  Dietary Fiber: **9.4 g (38%)**
  Total Sugars: **54.18 g**

Protein: **10.46 g (19%)**
Vitamin A **12892 mcg (553%)**
Vitamin C **77.1 mcg (103%)**
Vitamin D **87 mcg (15%)**
Potassium **1198 mg (25%)**
Calcium **439 mg (44%)**
Iron **1.53 mg (9%)**

Kiwi Orange-Flower Smoothie

Makes 2 servings

PREP TIME: 10 minutes • **COOK TIME:** 0 • **TOTAL TIME:** 40 minutes
Level 1: Very Easy

The next time you crave a tropical vacation, save the money, and make this smoothie instead! Fresh kiwis blended with aromatic orange-flower essence, sweet pineapples, creamy bananas, and savory basil, give every sip of this smoothie a refreshing burst of flavor.

INGREDIENTS

- 5 kiwis, peeled and chopped
- ½ cup pineapple, chopped*
- ¼ cup basil leaves, loosely packed
- 1 banana
- 2 tablespoons orange-flower essence
- 1 tablespoon sesame seeds

INSTRUCTIONS

1. Combine all Ingredients in a blender except sesame seeds, and process until smooth.

2. Refrigerate for at least 30 minutes, until cool.

3. Pour into two glasses and top each with half of the sesame seeds before serving (optional).

NOTE: *Use fresh, frozen, or canned pineapple.

NUTRITION • PER ONE SERVING

Calories **190 (9%)**
Total Fat **3.7 g (6%)**
  Saturated Fat **0.52 g**
  Polyunsaturated Fat **1.67 g**
  Monounsaturated Fat **1.18 g**
  Trans Fat **0 g**
Cholesterol **0 mg**
Sodium **8 mg**
Total Carbohydrate: **42.36 g (16%)**
  Dietary Fiber: **2.5 g (27%)**
  Total Sugars: **25.57 g (28%)**

Protein: **3.69 g (7%)**
Vitamin A **67 mcg (3%)**
Vitamin C **11.1 mcg (15%)**
Vitamin D **0 mcg**
Potassium **321 mg (7%)**
Calcium **16 mg (2%)**
Iron **0.6 mg (3%)**

Green Kale Smoothie

Makes 2 servings

PREP TIME: 12 minutes • **COOK TIME:** 0 • **TOTAL TIME:** 42 minutes

Level 1: Very Easy

If you're not a fan of green smoothies, this recipe will make you rethink that choice! The combination of Ingredients also creates a vivid flavor, perfect for waking you up in the morning. Packed with calcium, vitamin C, and anti-oxidants, this is a fueling beverage.

INGREDIENTS

- 1 cup almond milk, chilled
- ½ cup chopped kale leaves
- 2 large broccoli florets, chopped
- 1 stalk celery, roughly chopped
- ½ green bell pepper, seeded and chopped
- 1 tablespoon ginger, peeled and grated
- Juice of 1 lime

INSTRUCTIONS

1. Combine all Ingredients in a blender and process until smooth.
2. Refrigerate for at least 30 minutes, until cool.
3. Pour into two glasses and serve.

NUTRITION • PER ONE SERVING

- Calories **136 (6%)**
- Total Fat **4.69 g (10%)**
  - Saturated Fat **2.378 g**
  - Polyunsaturated Fat **0.501 g**
  - Monounsaturated Fat **1.306 g**
  - *Trans* Fat **0 g**
- Cholesterol **12 mg**
- Sodium **98 mg (7%)**
- Total Carbohydrate: **18.85 g (8%)**
  - Dietary Fiber: **1.3 g (5%)**
  - Total Sugars: **7.08 g**
- Protein: **8.63 g (16%)**
- Vitamin A **2469 mcg (106%)**
- Vitamin C **218.7 mcg (292%)**
- Vitamin D **2 mcg**
- Potassium **733 mg (16%)**
- Calcium **230 mg (23%)**
- Iron **1.55 mg (9%)**

Watermelon Lime Drink

Makes 15 servings

PREP TIME: 15 minutes • **COOK TIME:** 0 • **TOTAL TIME:** 15 minutes
Level 2: Easy

The secret ingredient in this refreshingly sweet beverage is the earthy and peppery sage. If you're new to using agave nectar as a sweetener you are in for a surprise, as it's not only plant-based, it's also low on the glycemic index and won't spike your blood sugar.

INGREDIENTS

- 10 cups watermelon, cubed
- 1 cup cold water
- ¼ cup freshly squeezed lime juice
- ¼ cup sage leaves, packed
- 2 limes, cut into wedges
- 1 tablespoon agave nectar

INSTRUCTIONS

1. Add the watermelon to a blender in batches and process until liquefied.

2. Pour the watermelon liquid through a fine-mesh strainer set over a large bowl and strain until only the pulp remains.

3. Transfer the strained juice to a pitcher, stirring in the water and lime juice, and refrigerate.

4. Muddle the sage, lime wedges, and agave nectar in a small bowl, until fragrant.

5. To serve, put a teaspoon of the muddled mixture in tall glasses, add ice if desired, and pour in the watermelon juice. Stir to combine. Refrigerate leftovers in an airtight container for up to 3 days.

NUTRITION • PER ONE SERVING

Calories **59 (3%)**	Protein: **1.21 g (2%)**
Total Fat **0.35 g (1%)**	Vitamin A **1069 mcg (46%)**
Saturated Fat **0.067 g**	Vitamin C **17.9 mcg (24%)**
Polyunsaturated Fat **0.102 g**	Vitamin D **0 mcg**
Monounsaturated Fat **0.078 g**	Potassium **222 mg (5%)**
Trans Fat **0 g**	Calcium **28 mg (3%)**
Cholesterol **0 mg**	Iron **0.61 mg (3%)**
Sodium **3 mg**	
Total Carbohydrate: **15.01 g (6%)**	
Dietary Fiber: **1 g (4%)**	
Total Sugars: **11.45 g**	

Red Pepper Berry Smoothie

Makes 4 servings

PREP TIME: 12 minutes • **COOK TIME:** 10 minutes • **TOTAL TIME:** 52 minutes
Level 2: Easy

It's hard to believe that cauliflower is the secret ingredient that creates the wonderfully creamy texture of this smoothie. Perfect to serve at a summer barbecue—since the fruits and vegetables will be in season—add this recipe to your al fresco dining list!

INGREDIENTS

- 2 cups water
- 1½ cups cauliflower florets
- 1 (32-oz.) carton strawberry Greek yogurt
- 2 cups frozen or fresh raspberries
- 1½ cups fresh strawberries, sliced
- 1 red bell pepper, seeded and cut into strips

INSTRUCTIONS

1. Add the water into a saucepan set over medium-high heat and bring to a boil.

2. Add cauliflower florets to the boiling water and cook for 8–10 minutes, until tender. Drain and set aside until slightly warm.

3. Combine warm cauliflower with the remainder of the Ingredients in a blender and process until smooth and creamy. Refrigerate for at least 30 minutes, until cool.

4. Pour into four tall glasses and serve.

NUTRITION • PER ONE SERVING

Calories **347 (16%)**
Total Fat **0.84 g (2%)**
  Saturated Fat **0.308 g**
  Polyunsaturated Fat **0.251 g**
  Monounsaturated Fat **0.111 g**
  Trans Fat **0 g**
Cholesterol **0 mg**
Sodium **92 mg (6%)**
Total Carbohydrate: **66.99 g (27%)**
  Dietary Fiber: **9.6 g (38%)**
  Total Sugars: **56.49 g**

Protein: **20.51 g (38%)**
Vitamin A **1013 mcg (43%)**
Vitamin C **110.4 mcg (147%)**
Vitamin D **0 mcg**
Potassium **314 mg (45%)**
Calcium **275 mg (28%)**
Iron **1.6 mg (9%)**

Pear Spinach Smoothie

Makes 2 servings

PREP TIME: 10 minutes • **COOK TIME:** 0 • **TOTAL TIME:** 40 minutes
Level 1: Very Easy

The flavor of this smoothie depends on your choice of pear. The Concorde and Comice varieties impart a sweet taste, whereas a Bosc or Forelle pear exude a tart edge. No matter which you choose, the natural sweetness of the dates still comes through.

INGREDIENTS

½ cup walnut milk

½ cup fresh spinach leaves, loosely packed

1 pear, seeded and diced

2 dates, pitted

INSTRUCTIONS

1. Combine all Ingredients in a blender and process until smooth.
2. Refrigerate for at least 30 minutes, to chill.
3. Pour into two glasses and serve.

NUTRITION • PER ONE SERVING

Calories **85 (4%)**
Total Fat **2.19 g (5%)**
  Saturated Fat **1.152 g**
  Polyunsaturated Fat **1.166 g**
  Monounsaturated Fat **0.529 g**
  Trans Fat **0 g**
Cholesterol **6 mg**
Sodium **32 mg (2%)**
Total Carbohydrate: **15.01 g (6%)**
  Dietary Fiber: **2.9 g (12%)**
  Total Sugars: **11.91 g**

Protein: **2.61 g (5%)**
Vitamin A **803 mcg (34%)**
Vitamin C **4.5 mcg (6%)**
Vitamin D **1 mcg**
Potassium **243 mg (5%)**
Calcium **82 mg (8%)**
Iron **0.29 mg (2%)**

Sweet Potato Orange Juice

Makes 2 servings

PREP TIME: 12 minutes • **COOK TIME:** 0 • Total Time 42 minutes
Level 1: Very Easy

Drink this juice to help support your immune system, promote gut health, and increase your energy level! How? It's all thanks to the Mediterranean favorite—sweet potatoes. What's more, it is a light and refreshing change from sugary store-bought OJ.

INGREDIENTS

- ½ cup orange juice, freshly squeezed (2 oranges)
- ¼ cup sweet potato, grated
- ½ red apple, seeded and chopped
- 1 carrot, peeled and chopped

INSTRUCTIONS

1. Combine all Ingredients in a blender and process until smooth.
2. Refrigerate for at least 30 minutes, to chill.
3. Pour into two glasses and serve.

NUTRITION • PER ONE SERVING

Calories **153 (7%)**
Total Fat **0.69 g (1%)**
  Saturated Fat **0.099 g**
  Polyunsaturated Fat **0.207 g**
  Monounsaturated Fat **0.079 g**
  Trans Fat **0 g**
Cholesterol **0 mg**
Sodium **45 mg (3%)**
Total Carbohydrate: **37.08 g (15%)**
  Dietary Fiber: **4.7 g (19%)**
  Total Sugars: **26.79 g**

Protein: **2.23 g (4%)**
Vitamin A **10916 mcg (468%)**
Vitamin C **94.8 mcg (126%)**
Vitamin D **0 mcg**
Potassium **681 mg (14%)**
Calcium **51 mg (5%)**
Iron **0.72 mg (4%)**